Poetry Behind Prison Bars

Set Yourself Free...

Jose M. Viera Sr

Janet M. Viera

"I have blocked most traumatic events out for my own sanity. Some days I wish I could block it all out however certain things like grief, will still linger. Then you learn the tools to help you process grief. Those tools lead to one of the greatest things that I am grateful for and that is the healing ability to speak upon it now without feeling shame, as if I was supposed to get over it anyway. Only one who has experienced this process, knows the courage and resiliency it takes to get to this place."

Janet M. Viera

ISBN: 978-1-7365499-1-9

DEDICATION

Jose: "This book with all its written material and work is dedicated to my parents, Catalino and Zoraida Viera whose character I took on throughout my life. In addition, this will go out to my lovely daughter Janet and my mirror image son Joey. As well as all those persons' whose inspiration and love prompted these writings and are not Forgotten......."

Janet: Ditto to everything my dad said, lol. My Abuelas prayers, my Abuelos wisdom and a lot of shadow work is what has built me into to Viera Strong woman that I am today. Those 2 deserve all the recognition coming to them from near and far. Although they aren't physically here with us anymore, however their spirits will always live in our big red Viera house, and their wisdom will forever live in our hearts. I would also like to shoutout my children Shadea, Tatyana, and RaSean. You guys have no idea how much you inspire me by showing me, well ME, lol. I love you. To my mom Sylvia Rowell, 2020 was one for the record books however I am so grateful that you have been there day in and day out as I was caring for Abuela and Abuelo. You are so appreciated. To my small circle of genuine friends who have become family, you have each been there for me whether it is a phone call, text, moral support, and I am so grateful for every one of you. I am so blessed to have you as family.

CONTENTS

POETRY BEHIND PRISON BARS

Set Yourself Free...

FOREWORD

Hello, my name is Janet, I have a new life in God, and I am recovering from Grief... A line I repeated every week for a whole year, as I was going through my programs. There were a few other things thrown in there as well, however Grief was definitely thee toughest because it seemed almost consistent throughout my life or at least so I thought. From the tender age of 5 when my dad was taken away to jail, to the two most recent ones being the most consistent, unconditionally loving individuals in my life being taken away, both in December 2020. I've had my fair share of grief; however, I am grateful to say that these were struggles, they were tools of shame that I allowed others to use against me, titles that I allowed to keep me in a stagnant state, these days they are part of my recovery. The reason I am as Resilient as I am today. These days I have the tools and a different perspective which allows me to push forward every day. My goal is to teach others these tools in order to help them overcome everyday struggles, as well as teach them how to be resilient in every aspect of life. This journey through grief was not easy, still isn't easy, however achieving a balance of peace is much simpler than we make it. Racing thoughts? Trust and believe with practice they can be silenced. Depression to where you can't function? I promise you will get up and live life again. Peace is achievable if you make the hardcore decision to seek it and practice it. Disclaimer: These are my personal experiences and how I have overcome them. Although I am a medical professional, I do not have a license to diagnose. Therefore, these should not in any way be taken as a means to diagnose or treat your own mental health. If you are in a crisis, please call the hotline at 1-800-273-8255

I AM GRATEFUL

This is where it all started Miguel Viera and Rosa Gomez were the parents of my grandfather Catalino Viera. Two legends in the small barrio of El Mango in Juncos, Puerto Rico. Many of days I remember walking inside Abuela Rosa's house and always smelling good Spanish food on the stove from early in the morning.

Abuela Juana Torres and Jose Torres were the reason my Abuela Zoraida Viera was here. She could cook but she also had the sweets on lock. The memory of her sitting on her patio eating pepitas are still vivid and bring me comfort ....

I am so grateful for my great grandparents who blessed me with my grandparents and my grandparents who blessed me with my parents. I am so grateful for the memories in Puerto Rico growing up. I am grateful for my whole team of guardian angels and all of their protection all around me daily, I Am Grateful to be blessed with a balance of a peaceful life, even in the storms. I Am Grateful, I Am Grateful, I AM GRATEFUL....

MY GREAT GRANDPARENTS IN PUERTO RICO: ABUELO MIGUEL AND ABUELA ROSA

MY BEAUTIFUL GREAT GRANDMOTHER JUANA IN PUERTO RICO

MY GRANDPARENTS ZORAIDA AND CATALINO VIERA.

MY GRANDFATHER CATALINO

MY GRANDMOTHER ZORAIDA

Chapter 1:

"Denial is the lid on our emotional pressure cooker: the longer we leave it on, the more pressure we build up. Sooner or later, that pressure is bound to pop the lid, and we have an emotional crisis."

-Susan Forward

I walked in the house and asked, "Where's my dad?"

Abuela says, "Que?" with a confused look on her face. Mind you this was back in the 80s, Abuela did not play that walking in her house speaking English crap, absolutely not, lol.

"Se fue pal el colegio," she said. She could not look me in my eyes. I may have been young however I realized early how gifted I was. I played the role though as I also knew my place!

I remember as time went on; I would overhear conversations about my dad. Never the whole truth though. Conversations would cease when I walked in the room. In this age they felt as though they were protecting me. Talking to my brother did not make things any better, we were both in such denial. We had that magical hope as children you know. We prayed to God every day to bring our dad home, yet no one answered. I would go to church faithfully with mis Abuelos. My grandfather was the pastor! I could not quite understand how this praying thing went. The more I did it and heard nothing, the angrier I got. "Isn't this what you want?!" I would yell out and silence would drop again...

(Translations: [1] "What?" [2] "He went to college".)

P.S.

It's not the crimes we committed

That constitutes the reason for our

Incarceration: It is our own stupidity

For getting caught the reason we are here

P.S. Does not concern the innocent…

Eventually I began bargaining with God. Saying things like, "I promise, I'll get better grades, I'll behave better... Bring my dad home Please." Silence... By this time, I was quite sure I didn't have this prayer thing right. Quite embarrassing for the pastor's granddaughter to admit...

Weekend visits began and let me tell you Abuela was faithful to her weekly visits with her son. She was faithful to making sure she took us to see our dad. She was adamant and determined to make sure we had a relationship with our dad. It hurt though, going to a county jail visiting our dad behind glass, talking to him on what looked like a pay phone. All we could do was match hands on the glass and imagine. That was hell for a little girl and little boy who just wanted to hug their dad. I couldn't fully understand what was going on, but I know I wasn't being told the truth. Eventually I began to refuse going......

"For every minute you remain angry, you give up sixty seconds of peace of mind."

-Ralph Waldo Emerson

"Vas a visitar tu papa?," Abuelo asked. I just looked at him. Several months had passed since I had seen my dad. I was definitely missing him, however the thought of seeing him in that state was worse for me.

Fighting over the remote with my brother, uncles and cousins became a regular Saturday morning routine. I always loved watching the karate movies with my Tio Luis but sometimes I did not want to watch wrestling. I wanted to watch Rainbow Brite. At this time, I was the only girl being raised amongst 7 boys including Abuelo. You learn a lot about men growing up in a house full of them. So, I was well aware that this was Abuelos way of causing a distraction, lol.

"Lo puedes ver en persona ahora?," he said. That intrigued me but I still answered," Abuelo, no lo quiero ver asi." I felt the sadness all throughout my body of seeing the pain in my dad's eyes and I would rather not.

"Yo sé que duele, pero tú eres una niña de fe, tú eres una niña de oración, y tu poder ponerte una sonrisa y irte a ver a tu papa. El te necesita." Abuelo said.

"Family first by any means necessary, even if it means you put your own feelings aside," I repeated in my head. Conversations like these would affect me for years to come. It began my overthinking processes, my inability to say no, as well trying to prove my worth to people, my people pleasing. I became fixated on being the pastor's "good granddaughter." Bottle it up, suck it up buttercup, became the norm, put a smile on your face and keep it moving. Being raised in a house full of males, I was expected to either man up or get trampled playing....

(Translations: [3.] "Are you going to visit your dad?" [4.] "You can see him in person now." [5.] "Grandpa I don't want to see him that way." [6.] "I know it hurts but you are a girl of faith, you are a girl of prayer, and you can put a smile on your face and go see your dad, he needs you.")

MILES AWAY

You hear the tone,

It flickers your heart,

A sound so near,

Yet far apart....

Sometimes it is the faint sound that she makes

You can hardly hear her, even if you hear every crisp sound.

What would it be like to not that sound on a lonely night.

To hear it whisper to you,

Like a soft wind between the stars.

The night is normal,

The sounds are many,

Yet you hear her lovely tone echoing through your ear.

Your mind is relaxed,

The moments are smooth

That sound so close, yet so far away.

What a sound of a sexy voice,

Near your ear,

Yet .... Miles Away.

Thank you AT&T for making that possible!!

I was lost in thoughts when the phone rang, "You have a collect call from inmate Jose Viera from Trenton State Prison, press 1 to accept the call," the operator said. I swear me and my dad had this connection where he just knew the right time to call, even when he knew I was upset with him. I hesitantly pressed 1 and waited for the call to connect. "I miss you," my dad's voice expressed the hurt. "I miss you too dad."

"I got approved for contact visits, come and see me, you can actually hug me," he said. My thoughts but I can't bring you home, you can't come to my school functions, dad this hurts, I don't want to do this, everything inside of me was screaming in pain. Yet the words that came out of my mouth were, "Ok I'll be there the next time Abuela goes." I felt defeated, I felt alone but it was my duty to be there for my dad, right? I had to have faith, right? I was praying girl, right? Check, Check, and Check!!!! I felt like a robot....

My conversation with my dad stayed with me heavy over the weekend. I was so heartbroken. I walked into school that Monday tired from lack of sleep, pushing to get through the day. During gym I asked for the bathroom pass, it was my way of escaping. I went into the bathroom and cried my heart out. I came out of the bathroom with my eyes swollen. I am walking to get back to class quickly, I look up and see Mrs. Ostrander. She was always walking the halls picking up kids and dropping them off. "What's wrong Janet?" she asked. "I'm ok Mrs. Ostrander," attempting to avoid eye contact. She quickly took me by the hand and led me to her room. The minute we were behind closed doors, it all came out. She comforted me, encouraged me, and handed me a composition book much like the one I'm writing in now. I reluctantly agreed to journal; however, I soon came to find out it was one of the most liberating things I could've ever discovered. From that day forward, no one ever saw me without a pen and notebook....

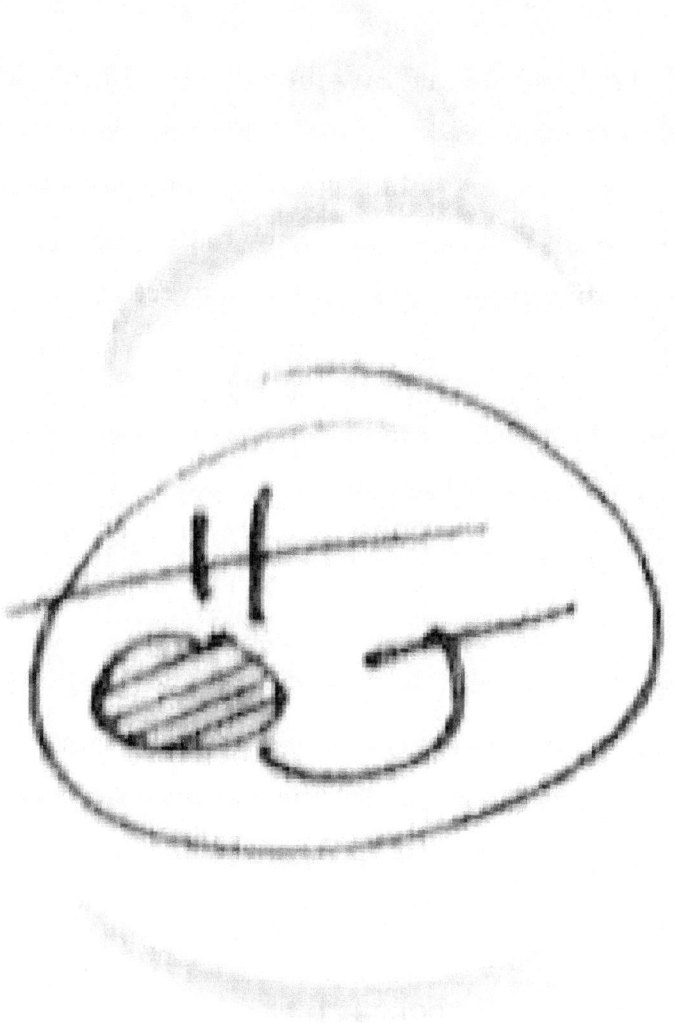

1-9-87

Dear JANET,

Hello baby. I hope you're Happy to get this Letter. I LOVE YOU VERY MUCH AND I MISS YOU!

I WANT YOU TO SEND ME SOME X-MAS Pictures of you and Joey by the <u>tree</u>! ☺

I hope you can come see me SOON. ARE you beiNG good iN school? How's grandmom and grandpop doing? WRite to me soon and don't you forget the pictures. Tell <u>Papito</u> he's my boy and don't get mad at me for not writing to him.

JaneT. MARIE Viera
Joey. Manuel Viera
Jose. Manuel. Viera.
4EVER ONE!

♡ Love Pappy

Joey Viera #2--
CN 861
TRENTON, N.J.
08625

PM
12 JAN
1987

TO: JANET M. Viera
P.O. BOX 256
Woodbine, N.J.
08270

Chapter 2:

"Bargaining with God is pointless, he already has a 1000 followers who will do what you bargained to do for free."

-Shannon L. Alder

Several years had passed and my relationship with my dad had improved. Yes, I still got in my shitty moods and refused to see him, he understood me and never took my isolation personal. I always kept the lines of communication open. I loved talking to dad about almost everything. He was the only man who ever seem to understand me.

When you are young one of our biggest misconceptions is that we have time, when in all reality tomorrow is never promised. One lesson I would teach my younger self is to cherish every moment as if it were your last. Because life is so unpredictable, and it just may be the last time.

TIME

What is time

Just ticking away,

Bringing memories

That passed away.

Why think of the past,

Or the last year;

All it could bring

Is a sorrowful tear.

In the glow of the eye,

The tear will shine.

That's what you'll get

When thinking of time.

Time is like something,

Or one of a kind;

That no man can change,

Or not keep in mind.

What is time?

If we want to know,

Time is a precious

Thing to let go...

Jose M. Viera Sr.

Angel Luis Viera and Janet Viera in Niagra Falls

You see this dumbo ears, kango hat wearing, breakdance looking mofo right here?! This is Tio Luis, aka Angel Luis Viera, aka Tio Super Lou the one and only! Lol.

My Tio really looked out for me. I remember him and D would bust out the cardboard boxes, the music blaring through old school boom boxes, and they would be out there breakdancing. Bringing small tastes of NY to Woodbine. I loved it. I loved spending time with my uncle.

We were closer in age, so we all grew up like brothers and sisters, well until I got in trouble lol. Tio was always around, so he and my grandparents took on being those figures, especially since dad was in jail and would be for a long time.

My uncle got himself a girlfriend and I loved her. Jeannie was all about family. It wasn't nothing for them to always have us around. Then he decided to date someone new, and everything changed....

"Death is simple the shedding of the physical body like a butterfly shedding its cocoon. It is a transition to a higher state of consciousness where you continue to perceive, understand, to laugh and to be able to grow.

-Elizabeth Kubler-Ross

February 1989 I could feel the anxiety high in my house. Abuela and Abuelo weren't home and all I was being told was, "Tio Luis was run to the hospital. He was hurt at work."

"The half ass secrets," I whispered to myself. I was only 9 years old but even then, I hated being played like I was stupid. I walked away, went up to my room and began to do what I do best.... PRAY!

"Dear God, please keep my uncle safe. Please heal him. Please give Abuela and Abuelo strength, please bring him home."

See at this time I had this crazy misconception that God was like tis slot machine in the sky. You know, just put a quarter in, pull the lever, cross your fingers, and hope something you want comes out.... Not too long after, I heard the commotion....

"¿Pero por qué Viera, porque Dios no sigue haciendo esto? ¡¡¡Primero nuestro hijo en la cárcel y ahora el otro hijo muerto!!! Ya no puedo, no lo resisto mas!!", she yelled. I heard her let out a loud cry of pain.

"Debemos que tener fe, Dios sabe lo que está haciendo." I heard Abuelo say. His voice was shivering, yet he would not shed a tear. I could tell he was questioning things too. However, his faith, not to mention his pride just would not allow him to show his emotions. In his mind, sensitivity was equal to weakness, and he was the man of the house, it was duty to hold it down. Emotions what are those, little did he know....

I came running out the room to find out what was going on. I naturally gravitated towards my Abuela, placed my arms around her and squeezed her

(Translations: [7]."But why Viera, why does God keep doing this to us? First our son in jail and now the other son dead!!! I can't anymore, I can't resist it anymore!!" [8]. "We have to have faith, God knows what he's doing.")

tight. "Abuela que paso? ¿Dónde está Tío Luis?' I asked.

"Tio Luis se fue a estar con Dios. Se lastimo en el trabajo." Abuela cried out. I sat there holding Abuela, as I silent, hurt and in shock. This was not happening again?!

Not too long after the house was packed. This was precovid so half the town was there. People were looking out for us, helping cook and clean, encouraging us. Unfortunately, I couldn't feel any of it. I heard the whispers throughout the huddlers of people Talking. "He was stabbed at the docks." "Yes, over the girl he was dating." I was walking around, hearing these things and began feeling heavier and heavier. At the tender age of 9, I had no understanding as to why I felt like I had the weight of the world on my shoulders, but I did.

That night after the house calmed down, I went downstairs to the basement and let it all out. I remember feeling so hurt and broken. I felt like I had finally come to a balance with my dad being gone to jail and then I get hit with this. Here comes the emotional roller coaster again.

"I began to yell out to him, "You couldn't wait until I turned the double digits. At least 10 Tio?!" My birthday is in two months Tio!!!" I cried and cried.

(Translations: [9.] "What happened Grandma? Where is Uncle Luis?" [10.] "Uncle Luis has gone to be with God. He got hurt on the job.")

MY TIO LUIS

ABUELA ROSA AND TIO LUIS

"Any energy you place on what transpired in the past is groundwork for guilt and ego loves guilt. Such negative energy fabricates an excuse for why your present moments are troubled and gives you a cop out, a reason to stay out of spirit."

-Wayne Dyer

Two weeks had gone by, we had buried my Tio, and it was time to get back to school. Abuelo was dropping me and Joey off. We get in front of the school and naturally Joey's hyper butt takes off running, "BENDICION," he yelled, as he is getting out the car. Abuelo just nodded his head and said, "Dios te bendiga hijo." I heard his voice cracking; I look over at him and Abuelo is crying. I immediately hugged him, and he held onto me for dear life, letting it all out. He found out later in life how grateful I was for that vulnerable moment. How grateful I was for the first time to see him cry. How grateful I was that God chose me to share that moment with him.

I came home from school that day to find out Abuelo had been taken to the hospital and he would be staying. All those feel-good feelings went away. Having my emotions pulled like that made me feel like I was being punished, I truly could not comprehend what I had done wrong to deserve all these heartbreaks. I went into my room, sat down with my notebook, and began to write….

(Translations: [11]. "Blessings." *This was the respectful way we were raised to speak to our elders. If you were walking in or walking out of their presence, you were expected to say "Bendicion". It was our way of respecting and asking our elders for blessings to keep us safe along our journey. [12]. "God bless you son.")

What Do We Do When the Pain Just Doesn't Go Away....

What do you do when the pain just doesn't go away?

Do you put on a mask and act as if it isn't there?

How do I "snap out of it" like they say I should?

How do I get up off this floor?

Do you just shut out the pain and ignore what's present in your face?

Or do you just use your imagination to take yourself to some other place?

Do you just let it rain?

In order to gain back who I am?

In order to grow?

In order to have wisdom learned?

Still what do you do when the pain just doesn't go away?

When you're struggling to write the final line?

So many unanswered questions,

Equates to confusion,

All this bottling it up,

Creates these nightmares,

I live them everyday,

As I ache to break away,

From this prison in my mind,

Find the peace that I visualized,

The clarity I envisioned,

I've come to this conclusion,

Create with imagination,

Numb the pain,

Cry your silent tears,

Mask away the stress,

Deal with the rain,

Allow your spirit to be cleansed,

All of this is happening for a reason,

God is working everything out in the end,

Without me having to put my hands into anything.

Janet M. Viera

Chapter 3:

"People who have never dealt with depression think its just being sad or being in a bad mood. That's not what depression is for me; its falling into a state of grayness and numbness."

-Dan Reynolds

My 10th birthday came but it was not really happy. I began to experience consistent sadness. This was 30+ years ago, so terms like depression, anxiety, isolation, grief could land you a nice little stay at Ancora Mental Hospital. I became withdrawn and even more quiet, but I continued to write. It was the only thing that gave me strength to put the plastic smile on my face and keep pushing through every day.

Time would go on, clothes and hair styles would change, puberty was a thing of the past and my freedom to go over my friends' houses by myself increased. This was a time where you could allow an adolescent to walk down the street alone. People all over town looked out for everyone's kids, it takes a village was really put into practice.

As for me I particularly enjoyed hanging out with older kids, it seemed as though they understand me better, not to mention you learned things ahead of time, which could be a good or bad thing depending, lol. I began spending a lot of time down the street from my house. My good friend was about 4 years older than me, and our friendship started off as like a big sister just looking out for me and my brother. We all just walked to school together and walked home because we lived on the same street. She made sure we crossed the streets safely and she just genuinely loved us.

I still clearly remember the first day she asked me to come over and play, I was so excited. She walked me home, asked my Abuela. Abuela told her to have me home before dark and off we went to her house. She had a boom box and tapes; you know the kind you had to take a pencil to wind back up if the boom box ate it??? For my readers who are scratching their heads at what I'm saying just Google it, lol... I was excited just knowing she was even allowed to play regular radio stations. Call me a corn ball if you so choose, however coming from a household where your Abuelo was a pastor and your Abuela the first lady, the only thing you were hearing coming from the old record player we had was Pentecostal approved Spanish music. Don't you dare think you were going to play that "worldly music" in their home!! Absolutely NOT!! It was most definitely grounds to get a chancleta thrown at you and she wasn't missing either, LOL.

Everyone in town knew Abuela who was as sweet as pie older lady, loved God and loved her family. However, they also knew Abuela had a very feisty side to her too, so she didn't play about either one of them. Hence the reason my friend always made sure to walk me home before dark, lol.

"The more you trust your intuition the more empowered you become, the stronger you become, and the happier you become."

-Giselle Bundchen

We began to get together at her house often. Me and my friend would make up dances in front of the mirror. We laughed and had so much fun. We made many memories, ones that will stay with me forever. I just loved how we genuinely looked out for each other. She had a heart of gold; however, I would soon experience the darkness that she had actually been living in for a long time.

After school games and activities were something, we enjoyed doing together. This particular day we walked back to her house, and I was over there for a while. We had lost track of time and the evening fell upon us quickly. Her dad offered to take me home because it was dark out. "Don't worry dad it's only right down the street, I can walk her", my friend answered him. "No, it's dark and if I take her home maybe she won't get in trouble." The look of terror on her face spoke to me so deeply, however she could not speak on it and that bothered me. We did not dare challenge it any further, we were kids. If an adult spoke, you listened, no questions asked.

I grabbed my stuff and we left. The feeling in my heart as I told her I would see her in the morning was heavy. I could not understand why I was feeling this way, I would soon find out though. We got into his car, I noticed he began to pull out the wrong way, but I said nothing, I was A KID who had been raised to respect my elders, what could I say?! He kept looking at me weird as hell. In my head I'm attempting to convince myself, it's my friend's dad, right? What is the worse that could happen right? My body was screaming otherwise.

He took a right turn onto Belleplain road, he began giving all kinds of compliments, licking his lips, that creepy molester uncle ish and I got shook. We ended up on a back road of a cemetery, hidden in the woods, and there is where one of biggest nightmares occurred. He touched me in places I didn't want to be touched, yet the fear paralyzed my voice. All I wanted was my dad. I strongly believe the combination of tears and my guardian angels is what stopped him from following all the way through with the act, however he had already violated me, the damage was done.

He finally got me home, much later than was anticipated however he managed to sneak that one by because my grandparents "knew" him or so they thought. He even managed to get me out of trouble.

Abuela was very empathic, not to mention the mother's intuition was always on high alert. "Hacen media hora que te fuiste de la casa de tu amiga. Ella llamo preocupado de ti. ¿Te veo esos ojos medio mojoso, estas bien?" she asked in a concerned voice. "Si Abuela, estoy bien. Quiero dormir. Te veo por la mañana. Bendicion" I responded softly and as normal as I could, but I know I wasn't fooling her. "Se Dios quiere. Dios te bendiga mi hija." I went into my room, picked up my journal and started with the word WHY. I wanted so badly to understand why I was so chosen to keep going through these traumatizing events in life.

I never called my friend back; she would've known right away something was off about me. And quite frankly I was exhausted from the fight or flight mode I had experienced that I just did not have the energy to talk. I fell asleep in a pool of tears, feeling angry, feeling disgusted, feeling like God didn't even care I existed, because in my young mind I was convinced that he would not have allowed none of these things in my life to happen, had he cared. I was so wrong.

"Why didn't you call me back last night?" she asked concerned. "Because it was late, I was tired, and you know Abuela wouldn't have let me use the phone." I answered tiredly. I barely slept the night before, tossing and turning in my bed. "What happened J?" she asked, insisting. "I'm too tired, I'll explain later." I answered. Her voice dropped and she said, "If you think I don't understand, I do. It's been happening to me for a long time."

I looked at the phone confused, "Your dad?" I struggled to ask. "He's not really my dad, he's my 0." "This doesn't make sense, please explain?" I was confused as all hell. "I'll explain later after we talk" she answered. I hung up the phone and the racing thoughts began.

(Translations: [13.] "It's been a half an hour since you left your friend's house. She called worried about you. I see your eyes are wet, are you ok? [14.] "Yes Grandma, I'm ok. I just want sleep. I'll see you in the morning. Blessings." [15.] "God willing. God bless you my daughter.)

"Racing thoughts begin when you lose focus of the present moment. Learn to refocus through various practices or those thoughts, will swallow your personality."

–Janet M. Viera

We got ourselves together and met up. Most definitely not at her house this time. I could never imagine myself stepping foot in her house again. Taking any chance of running into that demon, was not one I was willing to take.

"Again, what happened J?", she asked right away. I busted out in tears, "He took me on the back road of the cemetery..." it was hard to talk through the tears. "J you have to tell your mom. If you don't tell her, I will! It's been happening to me for a long time and every time I tell my mom she takes his side. She doesn't believe me, her own daughter! So please tell your mom. I'm tired."

Now I was angry at what I was hearing, her mom and stepdad? How could he?! How could she?! All kinds of crazy thoughts began to enter my head. Let's just say if my thoughts were on trial, I would be in jail. However, I was still a kid. "I don't want to do it by myself," I lowered my head in shame. "I'll tell her then; I can call her that way you guys can talk after I tell her." That was the plan, and I didn't know what to expect or how to feel. I just knew I had to do this for me and her, I could deal with the emotions later. Never did I think it would play out the way it did.

We both headed home and not too long after getting there, I put my earphones on my head and drowned myself in music. I was interrupted by my door opening. "Ven para abajo ahora. Tenemos que hablar." Abuela said. I looked at her face and could tell she had been crying. I get downstairs to the living room, it's her and my mom. My mom's eyes were swollen red, "Why didn't you tell me when it happened?" Abuela was pacing back and forth crying and praying, "Dios Mio dame Fortaleza." I was just stuck in tears; I didn't know what to answer.

37

Abuelo comes busting through the door with his work clothes on, shortly after. He hugged me and I could feel Abuelo shaking. 911 was called and they were at our house within time. I was escorted to our basement where I had to recount what had been done to me. I held my head down in complete embarrassment as I explained the details.

The more details I described, the angrier I seen my Abuelo become. Several state police sitting in the basement, and I heard Abuelo say in Spanish to Abuela, "Busca me la pistola, que a este lo vamos a buscar!!" My eyes opened wide, I was shocked, I did not just hear that out of my humble, calm Pentecostal pastor grandfather. Thank God none of the police spoke Spanish. Abuela had gotten a scary quiet. "Pues Viera se lo quiere buscar, no te paro. Pero te aviso que te calme, porque nadie más va pa la calce, pero ese demonio." Abuela was calmly crying. Now I'm looking at her for clues, normally she was the one needing to be calmed down. All I could see was her crying and continually closing her eyes to pray.

"What wings are to a bird and sails to a ship, so is prayer to the soul."

-Corrie Ten Boom

"No se lo diga a tu papa." Abuelo said. I was confused, what the hell do you mean don't tell my dad. This man just completely stole my innocence, that is the ONLY person I want to talk to right now!! But I respectfully responded, "Por qué Abuelo? Ese es mi papa. Él debe de saber lo que paso." "Pues mi hija, el ya está en la cárcel. Él ya tiene la mente llena de los problemas allá dentro. No quiero apurar lo más," he answered softly. "Está bien, yo no se lo voy a decir, pero Abuelo, ya tu saber que este pueblo habla mucho," I responded.

My Abuelo was doing nothing more than attempting to protect his son. I overstand this now, however at that time it was devastating to be asked to keep a major secret like that from my dad. Who the hell was I supposed to talk to about this???

The very next day my dad called, it was odd to because it was a weekday. My dad normally called on the weekends when he knew for sure we would be home. "What's going on mama?" he asked. He sounded stuffy, like he was struggling with allergies or maybe crying? "Nothing much dad, I was just sitting here writing in my journal." I just knew in my heart; he was waiting for me to confirm or deny if the rumors were true. "OK, is there something you need to tell me?" he pushed a little more. I just paused, and felt my heart breaking more. "How did you know?", I asked him. "I'm your dad Janet, and just because I'm in here doesn't mean I don't have other people looking out for my kids out there. I have ways of finding out what I need to know about my kids, you guys are still my world," he said. "Dad the person who did this was someone you knew, who was supposed to look out for me. How can I

(Translations: [16.] "Come downstairs now. We need to talk." [17.] "God give me strength. [18.] "We are going to find him." [19.] "Well Viera, if you want to look for him, I won't stop you. However I advise you to calm down because no one else is going to jail except that demon." [20.] "Don't tell your dad." [21.] "Why Grandpa?" [22.] "Well my daughter, he's already in jail. He already has his mind full of problems in there. I don't want to worry him more." [23.] "It's ok, I'm not going to tell him, but Grandpa, you already know this town talks."

trust anybody? Please help me understand." I cried. I could feel his heart breaking and I wanted nothing more than to wrap my arms around him.

It took the cops some time, but we finally got word that he was arrested. And it sure as hell didn't take long before the town began talking about what had happened. It began with hearing all the derogatory things that were said about me, which really stung because I always looked at myself as a rather good kid. I wanted to crawl in a hole and disappear.

However, what kept me going was that I also had many women coming to me encouraging me for having the courage to go through with having him arrested. Many of women and young girls alike telling me that he had done the same thing to them, and they were grateful I was fighting, they were grateful I was sticking up for myself, that gave me strength to keep fighting.

Nothing could fill the void of my friend though. I missed her so much. She still managed to talk to me at school during recess and we still have love for each other however it wasn't long before our friendship came to an end. I just pray that she never had to deal with that man again.

Interviews after interviews, court dates after court dates, counseling sessions, this seemed to be dragging on. Finally, we got word that he was found guilty and would be sentenced. Only to be hit with another brick, "supposedly" in the process he had become a confidential informant, so therefore he was given leniency and was sentenced to only 2 years' probation. I had been shamed, I had gone through so much stress simply fighting for myself, I lost my friend in the process, and all he got was a few years' probation. I lost faith in the justice system then, I got angry as hell and began rebelling.

Who wouldn't after having to endure such traumatic experiences since young? I felt absolutely justified in my anger, rebellion and resentments. And it showed through every one of my actions..

"There is no greater agony than to bearing an untold story inside of you."

Maya Angelou

Jose M. Viera aka "The Fonz"

My Life In Poetry...

I was once a kid with no knowledge of crime,

I played in the sun for days at a time,

I left the Big Apple, a city of freight,

and came to New Jersey to grow over night.

I started with smoking and then went to pot,

Then began the dealing and just couldn't stop,

My parents were Christians and church is their thing,

I wanted to be Boss, I wanted to be King.

So, I went further out to see what I could find,

I found a bunch a pill to really blow my mind,

I then went to shooting which really wasn't my style,

but found out the drug was stronger and the high would last a while.

I found entrapped with a monkey on my back,

and then came the stealing to keep myself on track,

I met a couple of so-called friends, which I thought they were cool,

They said come on Joe lets go do a crime and I went like a fool!

I should've thought of all the things that MAMA used to say,

"Be good my little Joe and never go astray."

I never really listened until the day I fell in jail,

and knew the crime was serious because I couldn't make bail.

I now have a lot of years, which half I have to serve,

I hate the idea of being here it's getting on my nerves.

I want to cry sometimes and cannot find the tears,

From all this anger in my heart and all these damn years!!!

I'm going to warn my brothers about the world in here,

and hope to God they take the advice, and never fall in here.

Jail is a place of terror,

Jail is a place of crime,

Jail is a place to be renewed, while doing all your time.

WHEN I come out of jail, I hope the world has changed,

because the life I had was really bad and now I want it all to go away.

The best things in life aren't free,

but the best thing in life is to be free!!!!!!!!!!!

By: José M. Viera Sr.

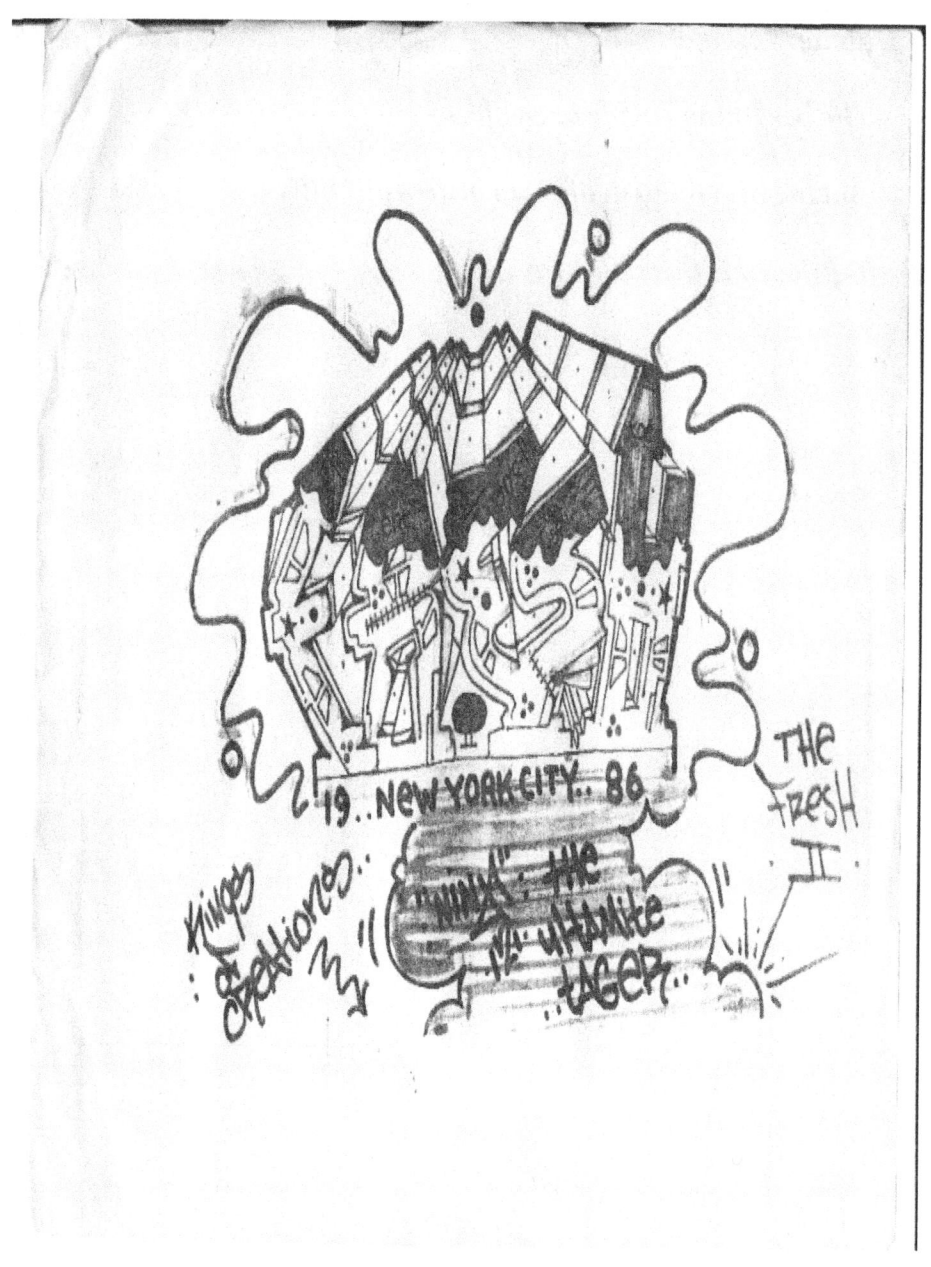

Picture by: Jose M. Viera Sr. New York City Graffiti 1986

Old school backdrop art created by my dad Jose M. Viera Sr. while incarcerated. Oh and I heard the crazy pins were back out again, so why not give you guys a good laugh, LOL

Chapter 4:

"Mental pain is less dramatic that physical pain but it is more common and also more hard to bear. The frequent attempt to conceal mental pain becomes a burden. It is easier to say, "My tooth is aching," than to say, "My heart is broken."

C.S. Lewis – The Problem of Pain

Growing up in a Pentecostal household you were sheltered from the world. We were raised going to church three times a week faithfully. You were led to believe that God was this outside source that you prayed for everything in your life.

One thing I will always remember Abuela saying, "Aunque los problemas vengan, pon se los en las manos de Dios, ponte una sonrisa y enseñarle al mundo que tú tienes fe y fortaleza." Unfortunately, the lesson I learned in it was put a plastic smile on your face and keep it pushing. It was hard for me to grasp that concept when I spent so much time trying to hide how I really felt.

In the years after that traumatic event, I lost my Tio Negro, my Titi Gea, my Abuela Virginia Gomez, my mom and dad had gotten a divorce. Mom moved out of my grandparents' house, and I chose to stay with them. Then mom had more kids. I then went to live with her and helped with my brother and sister. It seemed like I could not catch a breath of fresh air, to be a kid from the age of 9 and up. I stopped going to church and became very mouthy. Acting up in school, grades were suffering. I was being just plain disrespectful. Yet nobody knew that I was just sick and tired of being sick and tired of holding it all inside and carrying it on my shoulders.

I was still being taken to counseling sessions, but I felt nothing. Simply because I didn't feel comfortable enough to share my true emotions, I didn't trust. I felt like my trust had been broken by everyone I cared about, it seemed like everyone I loved and trusted either hurt me, died or left. I was talking to this invisible being in the sky and wasn't getting any responses. The only thing that brought me any slight comfort was writing and listening

(Translations: [24.] "When the problems come, put it in God's hands, put a smile on your face and show the world you have faith and strength.")

to music. I turned to everything that would make me numb from the pain inside. I don't care what it took.

."I've come to this conclusion,

Create with imagination,

Numb the pain,

Cry your silent tears,

Mask away the stress,

Deal with the rain,

Allow your spirit to be cleansed,

All of this is happening for a reason,

God is working everything out in the end,

Without me having to put my hands into anything."

Janet M. Viera

It slowly crept up on me yet happened so swiftly all in the same moment. Everything, Every, Last, Thing they said about me, became my reality. I wasn't aware enough to see the damage I was causing myself. I had a boyfriend, I started drinking 40s of Olde English, Steel Reserve, Mad Dog 20/20, smoking cigarettes, bud, sneaking out to parties, doing all the things a teenage girl should not have been doing, I was acting out big time.

Me and my brother began taking cars out for joyrides. We were definitely wild for this, but the memories we made were hilarious. Now that definitely wasn't the case in the moment.

My Abuelo and Abuela had this tan van, to them it was their mini-RV, lol. It was the place we created many memories with our cousins and friends traveling to church, traveling all up and down the east coast, sometimes I would use it as a hideout spot just to get some peace, quiet and write.

Los Vieras headed out to church.

*Exact replica clay vans my family owned, handmade and painted by Jose M. Viera Sr while incarcerated, simply from the pictures we sent him in the mail. Never failed to leave me in awe with the art he created *

They had taken a trip to Puerto Rico, which they often did, and they would normally go for a good while. The house was left open because we often stayed there alone, no worries about anyone breaking in because it was family all around.

My brother and I were a handful together. I had noticed they had left the keys to all the cars hanging on the key rack. I showed my brother Joey and he started right away, "Let's take a ride." The thought had crossed my mind too, but I did not want that whooping. "You're crazy, what if we get caught?" I answered. "J they are all the way in Puerto Rico. The rest of the adults are at a party, they are not worried about us." It did not take much convincing, the excitement of driving the van was overpowering, "Let's go." I looked to see this huge Kool aid smile come across his face, and I knew we were in trouble, lol.

We took a good look around to make sure no one was watching, got in the van, cranked it up and with my heavy foot we took off in no time, lol. We picked up so many of our cousins, friends and turned it into a party van. The music was blasting, we were having a good time, it was wild, the van was overloaded with people, and I completely forgot we were riding around Woodbine.

It was not long before someone called my family and told them they seen Janet and Joey pimping the Viera's van. We were oblivious to what was about to happen, "riding down the street, smoking indo sipping on gin and juice. LAIDBACK" Corny I know, lol but that definitely was the mood, until we got to the corner of Clay and Jefferson Ave, a small pickup truck smooth pulled in front of me cutting me off, I had to slam on the brakes, thank goodness I really wasn't going fast. My stomach dropped when I saw who it was, "Oh shit Joey, we are in TROUBLE!!" I yelled while laughing. When I turned around and looked back, the van doors were both open and everyone flew out the side doors and were running in different ways. That van was looking like the clown car. I never realized we had gotten that many people in there, LOL. My brother Joey had hidden under the pull-out bed in the back of the van. They jumped in the van took over the wheel and began yelling at me. They turned around and my brother told on himself by peeking his head from behind the bed. He was being nosey, watching me get yelled at and giggling quietly. "Oh, you too, wait just wait." They yelled.

"*Direct your children onto the right path, and when they are older, they will not leave it.*"
Proverbs 22:6

When we got back home, we got our tails whooped so bad. Rightfully so, we knew dang well we shouldn't have taken that van. They thought they had a good chance with getting us "kids" under control by beating us. Taking that whooping to make that memory was worth it to me, LOL. The excitement was still there after the physical pain wore off.

It wasn't but a short time after, that the similar scenario presented itself again. My mom was working at the nursing home, her and friend would take turns carpooling since they had the same schedule. The night before I was talking to her as she was getting ready for the next day, I noticed she put her keys in the drawer under her clothes.

At this point, I was a young teen who had begun to date an older man. Just Lost. He lived approximately 25 minutes from where I lived. I wanted to see him. Forget the fact that I had never driven out of town, I wanted to see him, that was it! A little too bold for my age, however the determination was always there.

I went into my brother's room and whispered, "We're taking a nice little ride tomorrow… Ahhhh hell, there goes that Kool aid smile again, lol." I walked out his room and went to bed all too happy.

We woke up and mom was gone to work. I went straight into her room and checked for the keys; they were still there. I started happy dancing all over the room. Joey called his friend to ride along. We knew she wouldn't be home until 3:30pm so we would just make it back before then, cool, no sweat. We got dressed, I grabbed the keys and out the door we went.

My mom had this pretty four-seater Camaro; we were all too excited for the ride. We get outside, turn on the car and the gas tank is empty. My heart sank, I had just called him to tell him we were on the way and now this. These are the days I wish I would've listened to Abuela when she spoke upon the paying attention to the signs, signals, and messages we were sent.

Instead, I looked at my brother and asked him, "What are we going to do now?" He sat quietly thinking then jumped out the car and said, "Come on!" We went in the house and literally shook down the couches, looked for change everywhere, cleaned out all the change we could find in the car and counted it.

Where there's a will there's a way, lol. We managed to gather up about $5-6 in change. Enough for some gas and the toll we had to pay. We locked the house door, and it was pedal to the medal.

We made the ride, picked him up. We were headed back, and I was literally right around the corner from our house when I see the red and blue lights. My eyes opened wide, and I heard my brother say, "Just act as normal as possible." Three teens and one adult in the car all with no license, sure buddy. I sure picked praying right back up in that moment. "God PLEASE!"

It was nobody but the grace of God that got us out of that mess. I looked older so they believed I was that person and I got off with nothing but a warning. Instead of being relieved, I felt the need to look up and say, "Oh this time it worked right?" in a disgusted tone, speaking upon the countless times I had prayed for more important things with no answer or maybe I never noticed. Nonetheless, I should've just kept my mouth shut, because I would very soon be shown that my words are much more powerful than I could imagine.

We looked at the time and realized it was only around 230pm, mom wouldn't be home until 3:30pm so we can get this car back and be cool. The officer turned around and went right after another car and I headed home.

We pulled up into the driveway just a few minutes later. "Joey didn't we close and lock the door?" My brother looked and his face turned white as a ghost. My mom came flying out the door and she was pissed. She just so happened to have taken a half day to take care of some things and comes home to her car missing. We got our tails whooped again, took it like champs and were placed on punishment.

Unfortunately, the fact that many of my loved ones failed to realize was, that the daily task of hiding the emotional pain I was carrying was way worse than any physical pain could ever bring me. No one could be harder on me than me.

WISH

Wish is a word,

That means a dream,

A something wanted

But never seen.

Wish is said,

A billion times a day,

Not ever really noticed,

That's its always in our say,

We wish for life,

We wish for money,

We wish for girls or guys

To be our honey.

Wish is a word,

That hurts so much,

When not succeeding,

Or not enough,

Why do we wish ?

Is such a good question.

So hard to answer.

Hardly mentioned.

As if an explanation is needed.

What wish really means.....

Wish

Is

Something

Hoped For...

By: Jose M. Viera Sr.

Running the streets and being grown led to fatigue and morning sickness. I was completely clueless as to why I was feeling nauseated all the time. It wasn't until my high school health class that I began to piece together what might be happening. After class I went to my friend and said, "I think I might be pregnant." Her mouth dropped, "Did you take a test?", she asked. "No, I missed my period, I been falling asleep everywhere, and I feel nauseated. I don't know what to do." I answered anxiously. "You have to take a test. Remember they mentioned it's a clinic next door and they do pregnancy tests without your parents having to sign. Make an appointment right at last period. You can sneak out and be back before the bus leaves to go home," she said.

Last period came, I propped open the back door and headed to the clinic. The only thought that kept repeating in my head was God please don't let this be true. Please allow it to be negative. I'm tired.

Chapter 5

"No one could be harder on me than me. My nightmares did not end when I opened my eyes in the morning, they began. Somehow, I had become accepting that this was life, until I learned some of the healing tools that helped me create beautiful dreams with my eyes open. Never underestimate the power of a pen and paper."

-Janet M. Viera

As a little girl I loved everything church. I loved singing, serving, praising, going to the sinagoga in NY, participating in youth bible camps, visiting other churches. I was about that Life, you hear me, All about it. I had many good times, made some great memories, met some genuine hearted people, some who are still in my life today.

However, by the time I hit those teenage years, the grief and sadness had been introduced to me throughout life so heavily, that I was questioning everything about religion, church, "Jesus", God, all of it. I still had hope and faith I just could not figure out where it was coming from. I maintained my sanity by still writing. Thoughts, ideas, poetry, dreams, goals, my journal knew everything. I became obsessed with wanting to know why I felt so out of place, in a place I grew up in.

My curiosity peaked research into different religious practices and cultures. I began visiting different religious churches in and out of town. Methodist, Catholic, Baptist, other Pentecostal churches, etc. I joined all kinds of groups. All I was trying to do was find my place in this world. Certain things I found weird, others I enjoyed, others made me think deeply, others inspired me. Each one had a different effect on me. I knew things were changing inside of me, they had to change, it wasn't just about me anymore.

Look, Listen, Learn...........

You gonna be alright Kid,

The less of speaking contains less of explaining,

The less of explaining contains less knowledge,

The less they know about you, the better off you are...

LOOK.... LISTEN... LEARN.........

The phone was ringing, and my gut told me it was my dad, but here I go again, "God please don't let it be him." I really had this whole process backwards. It stopped ringing and silence. I thought nobody got it then I heard Abuela yelling, "Viera, cuelga el otro telephono, yo lo tengo abajo es Chelo." Take a deep breath Janet and prepare yourself.

My dad may have been in jail, but one thing he didn't do was allow those walls to stop him from digging in our butts when we messed up. A few minutes passed and I heard Abuela say, "Dios te bendiga mi hijo, hablamos pronto." I swore I got off, I was celebrating all too quickly when Abuela yelled, "Janetcita, ven y habla con tu papa." I let out a long sigh, guess the praying thing didn't work this time either, I rolled my eyes as I walked downstairs.

"Hey dad." I said reluctantly. "Oh, we're an original gangsta now?! What is wrong with you and your brother?! Are yall both trying to be sitting next to me???" I became quiet, what could I say, we were wrong, and I wasn't about to be sitting here denying that fact. "What is going through yall heads? Do you realize you could've been arrested and charged? Answer me when I'm talking to you.?!", he yelled.

(Translations: [25.] "Viera, hang up the upstairs phone, I got it downstairs, it's Chelo." [26.] "God bless you my son. We'll talk soon." [27.] " Janetcita come talk to your dad.")

I mean from the looks of this picture, ummm I would have to question it, we kinda resemble the mob bosses' kids, I'm just saying, LOL. Those two very signature Viera smiles together, meant double trouble

I really hadn't taken that into consideration. Never had it crossed my mind that we could've been arrested when we got stopped. "Dad we were bored, and I wasn't thinking. I apologize." I answered lowly. He heard it in my voice, he was my dad, I couldn't hide it from him no matter how hard I tried.

"What's on your mind?" he asked. I heard the phone click on the other end. I knew either Abuela or Abuelo picked up the phone upstairs and were listening in, privacy??? Absolutely not in the Viera household. "Dad I just need to talk to you, unfortunately I grew an extra pair of ears, so it has to be in person. I'll come visit soon." I said. I was grateful my grandparents didn't understand our crazy English metaphors. He started giggling on the other end, "Copy that Teddy Bear." I began laughing, it was the first time in a while since I had laughed, and it felt good.

"Laughter is a beautiful blessing."

It had been several months since I had seen my dad, so I was happy to be visiting him. As I got older, I hated going to the prisons more and more. Because I was built like a woman, I was patted down and searched like a woman, yet I was only a young teenager. After waiting for hours while the whole line was registered, we then would have to wait in line while everyone got patted down and belongings searched.

It had been hours by the time we got into the visiting hall, and I was in a mood. My emotions were scrambled, and I was trying hard to keep them in check. However, when I see my dad coming out the back hallway with that huge smile, it was a knowing that everything was going to be ok. I mean this was the best place to tell him, right? At least I was protected all around by

71

CO's, right? I was so young and not ready.

After talking with my grandparents for some time he said, "Come on kid, let's go for walk." Attached to the visiting hall was a picnic area, when it was nice outside, we could sit out there. If the weather wasn't good then we would do laps around the gym, in order to get our private talks in.

Background artwork created by my dad Jose M. Viera Sr.

"What's on your mind kid? You've had me worried.", he said. I broke down and let it all out. "I'm tired of missing Tio, I'm tired being looked down upon like I'm just a trouble child, I'm tired of being the daughter of a convict, I'm tired Dad." I cried. "I promise it will all be over soon. I will be home soon. In the meantime, I need you to dry those tears up, have faith and continue to be strong like we have taught you", he said.

Yup, suck it up, bottle it up whatever you have to do buttercup, that was a solution that didn't seem to be helping me whatsoever but keep trying anyway Janet. How could I blame him, he was only teaching me the lessons he knew, and he was still learning himself.

"Soon is a few months, not years. I need you now, your grandbaby needs you now, I'm pregnant Dad," I continued crying. His whole aura switched very quickly, and a look of disappointment just came over his face. His baby girl was having a baby and I felt like I had completely let him down.

Telling the rest of the family brought different responses, mom and Abuela cried, my Abuelo was so disappointed and then my brothers and sister were all too excited to have a baby around. I was 15, pregnant, my whole life ahead of me, I didn't know how to feel. I mean I had experience with my brother and sister, but it was a totally different scenario when it was yours.

When I told my mom who the father was, she became incredibly angry. She was fed up; I mean who could blame her. She packed my bag, put me in that pretty Camaro and we went for a ride. Twenty-five minutes later we pull up behind my boyfriend's apartment building. I just knew this was going to be ugly.

The long stairs up to the main door felt like a walk of shame. I was hoping he wasn't home but halfway up the stairs, my heart dropped when I heard his music blasting. Just by that, I already knew he was drinking and that was never a good thing. He seen us as we walked to the open door. Rushed to cut off the music, put away his bottle and attempted to be respectful. My mom walked in, dropped my bag and said to him, "I asked you to leave my daughter alone, since you want to be running around getting young girls pregnant, then you can take care of her! And you, if you want to be running around being all grown, then get out here in the world and be grown because I'm not raising grandchildren!!" I was shocked at what I was hearing. I knew the intention was to teach me a lesson, but instead I grew more resentment. Hurt people, hurt people and I reacted with the first thing I knew would hurt her back. "I wouldn't expect you to, you barely raised us!", I yelled back at her. She left hurt and heartbroken, while I stayed behind feeling angry and justified in my response. As soon as that door closed, I changed again.

Whatever he was going through earlier was turned onto me. I never played about the disrespect. I grew up in a house full of boys, try me was my attitude. It seemed like it went on for hours though. I was relieved when he finally got tired and left. I balled up in the corner, bruised up, feeling angry and abandoned.

"*Hija fuiste, madre seras, como lo hiciste así te lo harán.*"

Translation: "Daughter you were mother you will be as you did so they will"

Although they weren't smooth, those nine months did seem to fly by, before I knew it, my baby was overdue, and I was waddling around trying to get her to come out already. "Drink some olive oil, or karo syrup," Mom said. "No, them two mother fu**kers need to go get some in. That'll make her go right into labor," Pops yelled from the kitchen jokingly. We all busted out laughing. Everyone had their own home solutions. It was the end of August, I was nine months pregnant, huge and it was too hot, I was willing to try anything to not be pregnant anymore, lol.

My mom went to the next appointment with me. Although our relationship still had a long way to go, we were still civil. I didn't speak upon what happened that night after she left. I wanted her to be a part of my baby's life. And being a part of my baby's life meant being a part of his life because we were a family. If she knew what had happened, we would be back to square one. Man, how young, how dumb I was.

"Since your baby seems to have a stubborn streak already, we will be scheduling you to be induced," the doctor interrupted my thoughts. "September 7th at 7am, please arrive 15 minutes before scheduled appointment to finish paperwork prior to being given the medication. The process normally takes 8-12 hours, but we all know nature takes its own time so that is not guaranteed. Are we ready to have a baby?" he smiled. I wanted to say being 16 and pregnant is no happy ordeal. Instead, I just gave him a half grin back, this had become very real for me. I had turned 16 in April and in September I'm becoming a mom. Whoa!

We arrived at the hospital early on the morning of September 7th and got induced. This stubborn girl took 26.5 hours to finally come out. I knew things had to change, I was now Mom to a 8lbs 3oz beautiful baby girl and looking in her chubby face made me so happy. I wanted to give her the world, in the same breath I had no clue where to start.

I was not stable, in an unsafe and toxic situation, working a minimum wage job, how was I going to give her the world? I became determined and depressed at the same time. Somehow, someway, I was going to make it happen.

CHAPTER 6

*"I am making good use of my time and
with what I invest, so that I may be around
even after the final payment is made for this
Borrowed Time."*

By: Jose M. Viera Sr.

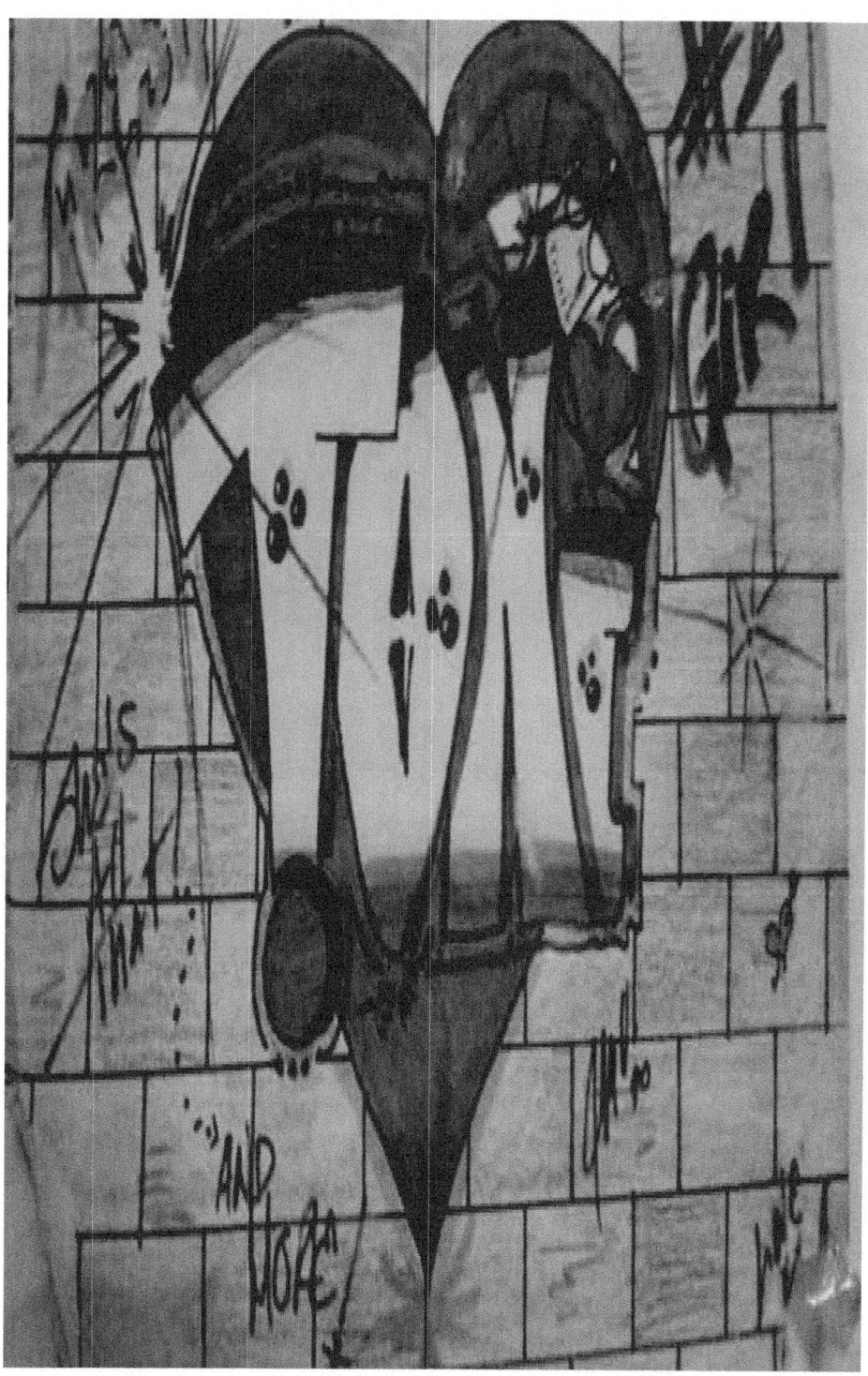

My dad looked so tired. "When are you bringing my granddaughter to see me?" he asked. "When you get out of this infirmary Dad. So, I need you to get stronger and go back out to population so I can bring her. What happened?" I asked him concerned. "My blood pressure was up, that's all. They got everything under control, and I'll be out of this infirmary soon." I clapped back, "Why don't I believe you?" he knew, that I knew something much deeper was going on, however he felt he was protecting me. These were the times I despised that just knowing feeling, I couldn't explain it.

A few weeks passed and we were able to finally go see him when he got out the infirmary, he came out the back struggling to walk. He immediately grabbed his granddaughter and began kissing all over her. It brought joy to my heart seeing him light up just by looking at her. "Let's take a walk, I want to take some pictures so I can show her off," he said. He had his own shoot with her, he was so happy.

On the walk back, I immediately asked him what was really going on with his health. He pauses, "I contracted Hepatitis in here. And they say my liver is failing and they can treat me, but I can't go on a donor list because I am in prison. I'm fighting for early release, but they have denied me twice. I'm just putting it in God's hands like Abuela tells us all the time. We have to have hope, and we have to keep the strong faith. It's what he wants," he responds.

Every emotion left my body after hearing that. I been serving God all my life, where is this good life he promises? If God was real, why does he just enjoy bringing me pain? God? I questioned everything about it. To me this God thing was the equivalent of being in a fight with Mike Tyson. You get happy as hell but for a few minutes because he swung and missed. But that next hit is going to land and will be even harder than the one before.

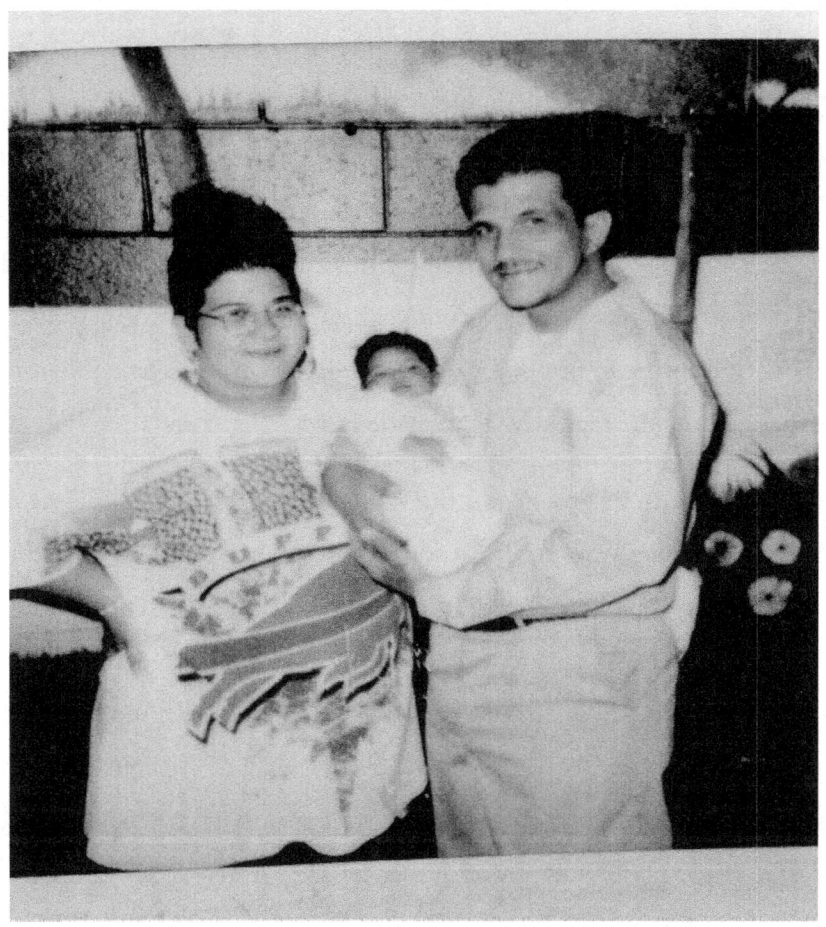

MY DAD, ME AND MY DAUGHTER SHADEA

That was the last time I seen my dad walking. He began declining more and more. He was spending more time in between the infirmary and the St. Francis medical center in Trenton, NJ. Unfortunately, they didn't allow small children to visit in those places so I couldn't bring my daughter. We had some pretty dope and deep conversations over those months. His wisdom and knowledge helped me slowly accept what was happening right in front of my eyes. "Dad I just want to be here. When you decide to take your last breath, please make sure I am here. I don't want you to die alone."

"I want to see my granddaughter," he said. I swallowed the lump in my throat, "Dad you know we can't bring her in here. It's not safe for you and it's especially not safe for her. She's already walking Dad." I tried changing the convo, but it didn't work. He's extremely unsteady on his feet, he's jaundice, and he is determined to see his granddaughter. He spoke with the nurse and got approved for me to bring his granddaughter outside so he could see her from the window the next day. That made his eyes light up.

The next morning, we made the haul to Trenton, NJ, this time with Shadea secure in her car seat. It turned out to be an extremely beautiful day outside. I left my daughter outside with family, as we got upstairs to my dad. He was waiting for us, ready to see her. We helped him up from the bed and held onto him as he took steps to the window. Once he got to that window, looked down and seen her walking on the sidewalk, he stood there watching her smiling and crying at the same time. After seeing her it was like he got a burst of energy. I got so happy and hopeful as if bringing her here was the solution. His early release hearing was in 4 more days. Maybe now he can get approved to come home and he will get better. Little did I know that this happens to a lot of people right before that moment they transition..

BORROWED TIME

"To be honest with you Mr. Viera you're living on borrowed time." The reality of it did not settle in. Borrowed time, borrowed time, I quoted such to family and friends like the latest released song on the radio.

I guess the tears accumulated with every playing of it. Finally, it hit me: "here I am feeling good, physically, maintaining mental strength and so forth, yet I am in debt with an invisible credit line and no money to pay.... to whom do I owe this borrowed time? When will he come to collect?"

I want to pay the man so my credit can be extended and flawless. The irony of it is he accepts no money, returned time, property or riches, he wants to be paid with your life!!!

Our most expensive asset is requested and taken as payment for our "Borrowed Time" we are using now. Do we cry, pant, holler or scream?! Or do we use it wisely? Do we use it to love, share and give? Or do we depress ourselves in self-pity, past times, memories, etc.

I am making good use of my time and with I invest so that I may be around even after the final payment is made for this Borrowed Time.

By: Jose M. Viera Sr.

"We have to get up the road to see your dad.", she said. "It's only 3 o'clock in the morning, why are we leaving now?", I asked. "Just get yourself together we have to go. I'll be there to pick you up soon." I jumped up from the bed confused, began to get myself together and it hit me, he's gone already. I can feel it and he didn't even wait for me. I became completely quiet. The ride to Abuelas house seems to take forever, I was stuck in a zone. By the time we got there the house was already full and I began to slowly feel the anger rising inside of me. Why would they lie to me??? I walked inside to a house full of crying people and my whole world fell apart.

In the days after I was completely numb. I couldn't feel, couldn't see, couldn't even cry. It was as if some unknown force involuntarily took away my ability to feel. How could he not wait for me??? Seem to be the only thing repeating in my head. I was in the front row of his viewing, just staring at his body. People coming up to me and offering condolences, and I could barely acknowledge them. I remember this one particular family member; she chose to look past the mask I had put on. She gave me a huge hug and whispered in my ear, "He will always be with you. It's ok to cry." Little did she know that was all I needed, permission. I was so used to bottling everything up, used to being so strong for everyone else, that all I simply needed was permission to feel. The tears began to overflow out of my eyes, and I became so angry.

After his funeral I got knocked off my heels drunk. By the time I got dropped off at home, I had a vengeance in every bone in my body. I began yelling out to my dad, "How could you not wait for me?? I knew you were going to die Dad, I just wanted to be there when you did! How could you not wait for me?!" I continued to yell at him until I got tired and fell asleep in a pool of tears. It's no deeper understanding than between a dad and his little

84

girl. Without him I was so lost.

ME, MY DAD AND MY LITTLE BROTHER JOEY, WHENDAD WAS HEALTHIER

Your brother has been taken to Albert Einstein hospital in Philadelphia. We have to get up there, pops is driving" mom said. Barely a week passed by that we had buried my dad and now something else, I was drained, I could barely function.

I was so grateful that Pops went with us and drove. It had only been a year since he and my mom were together, yet in that short amount of time he had already been a part of my daughter's birth, my dad's passing, and now he was driving us all the way to Philadelphia. He truly never missed a step; we were never his stepchildren and that's why we called him Pops.

Before I knew it Albert Einstein was within view, we pulled in and got into the hospital quickly. We got upstairs and were met with his team of doctors. The concerned look on their faces made all nerves begin to have a party again. You have to be strong for mom, get it together Janet. You don't have the time to deal with your own emotions I said to myself. Easier said than done.

"Your son is jaundice, we believe his liver may be failing and we would need your signature to perform the biopsy to confirm," they informed my mom of what the procedure entailed, and she signed the paperwork without hesitation.

When we got into his room to see him, I had a complete flashback. I was back at St Francis Medical Center, seeing a repeat of my dad. Yellow skin, weak, raspy voice and those eyes. Hold it together Janet, they need you. I kept repeating to myself. You don't have time to deal with your emotions, keep it pushing.

The procedure was performed at his bedside. They allowed us to stay with him for support and I'm glad they did, that needle was a beast. It took a few days for the results to come back, as the days progressed, he kept getting worse. Cross our fingers and let's try this thing again, "Please God not my little brother too, I need him, he's the only who understands." I pleaded.

After what seemed like forever, the results came back. "It has been confirmed that your son's liver is failing, we will begin further testing in order to place him onto the donor list immediately. He is going to need a transplant as soon as a match becomes available," the doctor said. Once again, I was numb. Like does this God person even listen, I thought to myself.

I lost track of time, I lost the present moment, and racing thoughts were inevitable. Exactly how much time had passed was not etched however knowing my little brother was literally within days of passing when a liver became available will forever be with me. Knowing someone had to die in order for my brother to get that liver weighed so heavily on my soul and heart as well. These were the times I disliked that I had such a big heart and felt things so deeply.

The surgery took a long while and after his recovery time we were told he was back in his room. Nothing they explained to us prepared me for the sight that I was about to see. "Remember he just had a lifesaving surgery; we have to keep him encouraged. He is not conscious; he will be kept sedated as the first 24-48 hours are the most crucial as we watch to see if his body adapts to the new liver. We will start removing one by one until he heals, you can expect his stay to be a minimum of 30 days," the doctor said. Blah, blah, blah, it all sounds like okey doke to me. My brother had gotten his liver and he will be home soon, that's all there is to it. I just wanted to see my brother.

We walked in there together and my little brother had tubes coming out of everywhere. Nose, side, mouth, breathing machine, what in the holy hell is this??? I expected to see him resting, I expected to see staples, I never expected this, I don't know what the hell I was thinking but it sure as hell wasn't this!!!

I felt like someone had just taken their Timberland and stomped on my heart with it. The room began to close in on me, this had to be another nightmare, I thought. The electric surges began in my body again, I had to get out of there. I got to go downstairs to get some air or more so vent into the air because holding it together was just not working anymore. I got to the side of building and let out a loud cry "Why would you do this to him? Why would you do this to us? My little brother is fifteen, FIFTEEN freaking years old, what the hell did he do to deserve this??? You just took my dad and now you're trying to take my brother too. Why couldn't you get my dad a liver too! What the F**K God? None of this BS is making sense!! I don't know why I'm talking to the freaking sky it's not like anyone's listening anyway," I yelled through my tears.

"He's always listening," she said. I had no clue who she was, I just remember her wearing a navy-blue scrub outfit, so I assumed she was a medical professional. "Who's always listening?! Because this person that my grandparents have raised me to believe in, just does not exist!!", I snapped back. I shocked myself when I heard myself say that. My Abuela would've had a chancleta at my head by now had she heard those words coming out of my mouth. "This is probably why he hates me so much," I whispered and hung my head in shame.

"Even though your thoughts are push him away, you can't because he lives in your heart, and he still loves you. Doesn't matter what you do he still loves you. Doesn't matter how much you yell; he still loves you. He's counting those tears and he still loves you. That pain you are feeling is preparing you for what's ahead. Did you ever think that maybe God sacrificed your dad's life in order for your brother to live? Everything happens for a reason, don't question, stay grateful for everything and just trust that he is always working miracles on his time," she said lovingly. Those words brought my temper tantrum to a halt, and the never-ending question part of the brain activated. Even though I had never considered looking it at that way, how come this lady was telling me he lived in my heart, when my Abuelo who has been a pastor for years told me he lives in heaven. Who was lying? I couldn't wrap my head around any of it, nor did I have the energy to even consider sorting it out. I was grateful and respected her outlook, however it was hard for me to feel her kind words due to the anger in my heart. At this point a miracle had to happen for me to believe this God person, wherever he lived, didn't hate me.

It was already embedded in my head that I wasn't leaving this hospital until he woke up. I managed to get myself together and get back upstairs. With my incognito cup full of liquor of course and a pocket full of gum and candy. Getting drunk became the regular, it was the only time I could forget about life if even for the moment. Forget about the fact that I felt so alone even though I was always surrounded by people. When I was sober the pain and grief was entirely too heavy to carry. I would zone out for hours, just lost in thought. Or spend hours sad and crying. Then I would place my plastic smile back on my face, and handle life, leading everyone to believe that I was good.

In my home, I was barely being able to function as a teenage mother. My baby girl wanting her Mommy, was only met with a shell of a person who just was not there. Then Mommy would take a couple shots and she was back to herself and happy again. Then fall asleep crying with baby girl in my arms, only to wake up still having to deal with the pain and reality that none of my loved ones were coming back. It was a pretty, toxic cycle that began in my life. And although I had seen stress being handled this way all my life, it was my fault and my fault alone for allowing myself to fall into this way of coping. I allowed my environment to teach me that this was the way to handle stress, when in my heart I knew different.

I hated living life this way, I just had no clue where to turn or what to do to change it. I am so grateful my family helped so much during this time with my daughter, and I am grateful she was too young to remember that time as well.

"Ask and it is given, Seek and you shall find, Knock and it shall be open unto you."

Matthew 7:7

"Papito stop trying to pull that out, Janet goes get the doctor!", my mom was yelling hysterically. My pops trying to hold his arms down, "This mother f***ker, strong as hell for just having surgery, damn!" This wasn't supposed to be happening, they said it would take at least 7 days before he woke up and was able to get that breathing tube out. I ran to get the doctor, "My little brother is trying to pull his breathing tube out!", I yelled. In just a few minutes his whole room was full of doctors and nurses, attempting to calm him down.

In less than 48 hours my brother had awakened and was attempting to pull his breathing tube out. They felt as though, "medically" he should be keeping it in longer, considering he just received an organ transplant, but my stubborn brother said, not happening. They had no choice but to remove it and he began breathing on his own right away. He tried talking right away too but his voice was too hoarse to get the words out. By the next day they had gotten a good amount of the tubes removed, he was determined not to stay in that hospital, for as long as the doctors recommended.

My brother went overboard, he amazed the doctors, when a little over a week later he was released from the hospital to finish his recovery process. Tears of gratitude, and tears of joy, covered my entire face. My little brother was bouncing back on that Viera strong wave. A little over a week ago this kid was on his death bed and now he is walking out the hospital. He is a walking miracle and that left me deep in thought, he saved my brother, maybe this God person did love me after all. The fire of curiosity in finding out the truth was lit again.

CHAPTER 7

"What we once enjoyed and deeply loved,
we can never lose, for all that we love deeply
becomes a part of us."

Hellen Keller

I was so grateful my brother's life was saved, that I actually began praying more often and making more efforts to visit church when I wasn't working. I still had so much confusion when it came to this religion thing, but I was attempting to sort it out. My biggest resistance came with the rules and regulations in religion. The conversations became deeper with my Abuelo as I was truly seeking my place in this world. Seeking understanding of various beliefs. Seeking where I fit with "God".

The more I sought the knowledge the more enlightened I became, soon after my dreams with my dad and uncle were becoming more vivid and descriptive. Sometimes I would have dreams of being a little girl again running around the yard with my dad, sometimes I would be riding dirt bikes with my uncle, other times they would speak to me, and the messages were unclear. It was weird at first but then I came to enjoy their visits to me.

One dream that kept repeating was of me and my dad's last conversation, where I told my dad I didn't want him to die alone. Then I would always wake up right before I could get an answer from him. That dream would wake me up in tears because I didn't quite understand death nor why either of them had to die so young. I would immediately start writing, it was the only thing that brought me peace. I had come to some acceptance of my uncle's death almost 10 years later. However, I was still so angry with my dad for not waiting for me and I wondered how long it would take for me to forgive him. That was the biggest factor for me, he died alone in a jail hospital. Not surrounded by the love of his family but ALONE. Why would anyone want to do that?

SOLITUDE

ONCE MORE I SPEAK WITH YOU MY FRIEND SOLITUDE.

AGAIN YOU HEAR MY CRY AND ACCOMPANY ME IN MY
SADNESS.

TELL ME YOU ARE NOT TIRED OF LISTENING,

I NEED YOU MY FAITHFUL FRIEND.

IN YOU I CONFIDE MY SECRETS;

MY TRIUMPHS;

MY FALLS,

FOR I KNOW THERE IS NO TREASON IN THE SILENCE YOU GIVE.

OUT OF ALL THE FRIENDS I'VE HAD,

NO OTHER HAS BEEN COMPASSIONATE LIKE YOU,

WITHOUT HATE.

YOU GIVE ME LIGHT

IN MY DARKEST DAYS.

FEELING YOUR TENDERNESS,

LIKE A MOTHER YOU HAVE BEEN.

YOU HAVE LOVED ME LIKE YOUR CHILD,

HOLDING ME IN YOUR ARMS,

WITH MY CHEST IN PIECES,

OF MY TEARS YOU HAVE DRUNK.

I CONFESS TO BE YOUR FRIEND SOLITUDE

MY PARTNER.

DON'T BREAK THE CHAINS THAT TIE US UNJUSTLY.

I AM AFRAID OF LOSING YOU,

I KNOW NOTHING MORE.

YOU HAVE SEEN ME ON MY KNEES,

IMPLORING UP ABOVE

FOR A BIT OF CONSOLATION

JOSE M. VIERA SR.

In that time, I was also diagnosed with diabetes. It was scary because my Abuela Virginia had many complications with her diabetes. The headaches and the mood swings were bothersome but, my determination to get my life together was obsessive. I stopped drinking, I lost over 100lbs, walked away from a 6.5-year toxic and abusive relationship, landed a full-time state job, and bought my first home by the age of 19. Nope I was not playing at all, I bust my tail off working double shifts 5 days a week to make sure my baby girl had everything she could ever want or need.

I left high school early and immediately got my diploma. So, landing that state job was a blessing and a curse. I had also enrolled in community college with a major in psychology. My plans were to get a degree, in order to stay and retire there. Growing up in an exceedingly small town, a lot of us were raised to believe getting that job was like winning the lottery. Some have made awesome careers out of that job, my Abuela retired from there, more power to them and may they be blessed. To some, it couldn't get any better than a state job. Respect to the people who have held it down there for years. I found out later that it wasn't for me and that it could get better.

I say it was a blessing, in that the job afforded me the opportunity to give her everything materialistic, however it was at the expense of my time. I justified working so much with the excuse that I had to care for her financially however I was really missing my baby girl. It began a painful tug and war within my own soul. I would take time off work and feel it in my paycheck, then I would put overtime in and miss my baby girl. I was caring for people at work, caring for people at home and began not caring for myself again. I had lost my step once again; my balance was off and the only time I had left for me was to sleep. With that depression slowly began to creep its way in through the back window and took over my life again.

"This isn't like you. What is going on?", my coworker asked. By the tone of her voice and her body language I could tell she was concerned and pissed at the same time. She was my work mom, and she really did look out by making sure I got all my overtime in good places. I had been missing in action for quite some time and really wasn't keeping in touch with anyone. "I was working so much, I just got tired mom. I'm missing baby girl, when I'm with her she's driving me crazy, and I want to go back to work. I'm missing my talks with my dad, I'm exhausted, overwhelmed and everything just feels like its piling up on me. I don't want to be grown no more!!"

She really started laughing at me. I just looked at her confused with my face all wet. "Being grown isn't everything you thought it would be, huh? Having to work hard to take care of someone other than yourself is hard, isn't it? You should have thought about that before you began acting grown. The only thing you can do now is process this the best way you can. Keep writing out your feelings, get them all out. Write letters to your dad he still reads them and can still hear you when you speak, he is always around you. No time for pity parties, you chose this life and were given this life because you are strong enough to handle it and you are more blessed than you realize", she said. She was hands down a no BS kind of lady and most days I loved her for it, today the truth hurt, and I respected her even more. So much achieved in such a short amount of time. We were really blessed, yet I had allowed the fog from the pain to blind me to the point where I couldn't see everything, I had to be grateful for.

Because I worked in town where my grandparents lived, I would get to see my baby girl during my dinner break. We would sit down with Abuela and Abuelo, break bread, right before they went to church. Nothing got by my Abuela and Abuelo, I swore they felt every one of their children and grandchildren even when we weren't there. Abuela had this uncanny ability to tell us exactly what was going to happen and how it was going to happen, without missing a beat. She would have dreams down to the detail, then we would see those exact things occur and we would be left in awe, just how the hell did she know and what deal did she make with God for all this information.

That day I came home for dinner, my Abuela felt everything shift when I walked in, "Bendicion Abuela y Abuelo," I said trying to disguise my voice and not get too close. "Dios te bendiga hija," Abuelo responded. "Que fuiste a la barra ante de llegar aquí?," Abuela snapped at me. "Janetcita deja las bebidas y el fumar también, no quiero que pierdas el trabajo bueno que tienes. Tú sabes que las bebidas y las calles no valen para nada, y ya no quiero enterrar más ningunos de ustedes. Pon tu vida en las manos de Dios, él te lo arregla todo. Ora por fe hija, para sigue en la lucha. Ven para un servicio con nosotros," she said in her feisty tone. When I Abuela would give me advice like this, something in my heart would say, "Listen to her." However, I was already too tipsy and so engulfed in my pain to really hear the wisdom coming through her words and I simply responded with, "Uno de estos dias Abuela."

I despised being sad and would seek every avenue to escape it. Smoke a couple doobs, drink a couple Michelob's, take a couple shots, all while sitting in the back dayroom. Whatever it took to bring the real and fun Janet out to play as often as possible. I picked up drinking often again, I stopped working overtime, started calling out, used all my time, started racking up unauthorized absence and eventually after almost 5 years, I had no choice but to resign from a job I thought I would retire from. It was devastating to me at that time. My whole world was falling apart yet, again and I felt I had no control over any of it, or maybe I did, had I just listened to her.

Finding another job came too easy, I literally walked into a nursing home and walked out with work, they were even willing to train me to become a certified nursing assistant. I was so happy to be right back and took that as a sign that maybe walking away from that job wasn't such a bad thing. Moving on to bigger and better, right?

I occupied my mind with more work, that became my new addiction. Work on the clock, work off, anyway that I could get it to take care of home. I still occasionally tapped a bottle here and there too, anything to keep the pain away. My schedule became so sporadic and seeing baby girl was hit and miss, especially with her and me both being in school. I became a CNA in little time and also landed a job that paid for my certified home health aide training. Yes, I bounced back, however instead of being excited and grateful, all I could do was wish my dad was here with me to see it all, he would be so proud. I needed my dad more than anything right now. I needed the love and understanding that only he could give. I wanted to make these memories with my dad so these were the times, I couldn't understand the words my coworker spoke, how I chose this life. I would never have chosen to be a fatherless daughter.

Bastard Child by Society

With this piece I hope you walk away from your seat knowing a little piece of my story

I know many will agree when I say growing up in life is hard….

Experiences in mine have left permanent scars,

You see with a papi behind prison bars……. I grew up very lonely.

If it wasn't for my grandparents, things would've ended differently. I appreciate all my grandparents have done for me.

I was named a bastard child by society….

Because my papi wasn't around "physically", Society tried to pin the title of "deadbeat daddy."

What they don't know is my papi was always there for me opening my eyes and mind to this messed up society. Most of the lessons I needed to learn he taught me, and he reminded daily how I would always be his #1 beautiful lady.

My papi was the only man who could read my soul without me even speaking which was a beautiful thing because I didn't always feel like talking. When I was suffocating, he taught me how to breathe and when my mind drifted off, he brought me back to reality. He pulled the wool off my eyes so I could see what others were blinded by so easily.

He taught me what to look out for on these streets

My papi could see through the mask I put on for the family,

Amazing how he always knew when I was hiding something,

He would sit me down at visiting and say to me "Slow down sweetie. Your life will be lived as it is meant to be. And I only teach you so much about these streets just so you don't end up like me......Locked down behind four walls that some days seem like they're closing in on me. Killing myself mentally because I am unable to see my baby girl mature into a young lady. That last thing I want is for you to be sitting here next to me or even worse 6feet deep. So please listen to me." And his words of wisdom have always stuck like a good song that's been placed on repeat. My papi was the only one that could lecture me because he had lived through all the stories.

And even with fall after fall my papi would show me how he would get up wipe himself off and remained strong all 13 years behind prison walls.

So, see I was named a bastard child but only by society because my papi didn't fit their profile of a good papi. But my papi was always there for me emotionally and mentally. Not a person on these streets that can come with any excuse. Because if my father could have a hand in raising me from behind a justice facility, literally, then there's no reason, no excuse. So, take me and my dad's story as an example of what it could be between you and your seed. My daddy still watches over me as the angel that stands beside me and my babies. And in my world, I will always be daddy's lil girl....... RIP papi. Love you!!!

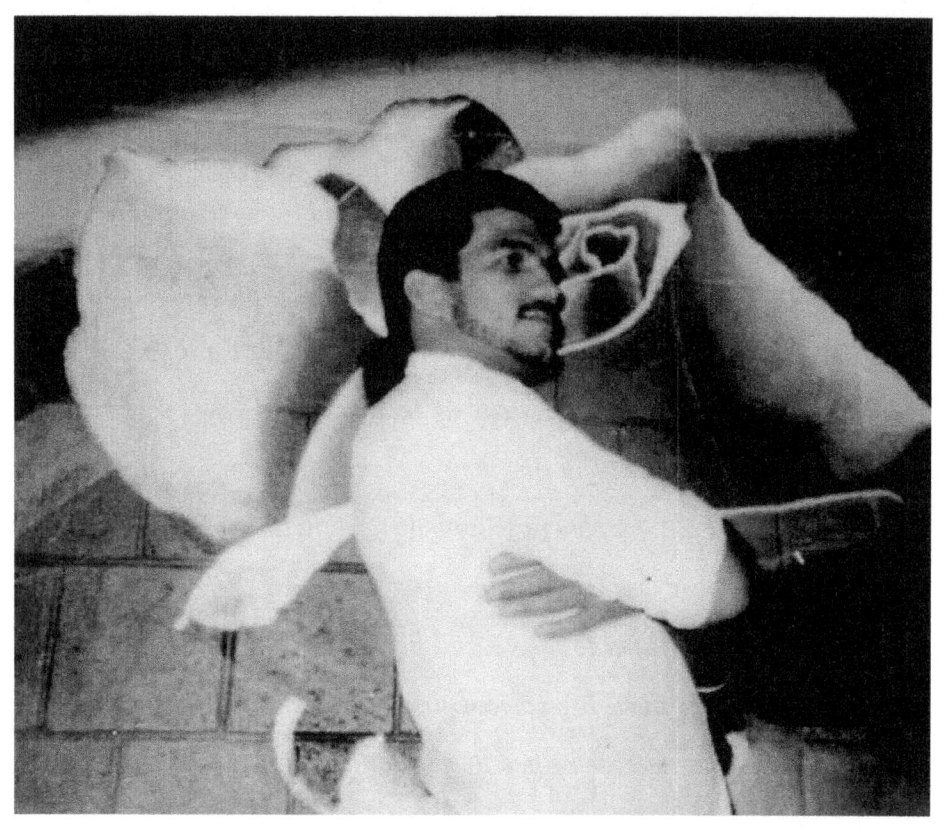

DAD WAS TOO COOL, LOL. HANDPAINTED BACKDROP BY HIM.

CHAPTER 8

"We cannot choose our external circumstances, but we can always choose how we respond to them."

Epictetus

"Red flag alert, red flag alert, RED FLAG ALERT!!!" I heard the alarms loud and clear, yet my response was hearts in my eyes, "Oh I Love him!" It seemed as though the more red flags I collected, the more "I loved him". I was so lost. I swear, if looking for love in all the wrong places had a poster board, my picture would be on it. No question about it.

Role play always came easy for me and I would without hesitation jump right into the wife role when I got into a serious relationship. All growing up watching my Abuela cater to my Abuelo's every need, did more damage than good. Please don't misunderstand it wasn't that she shouldn't have, it was the fact that I was missing the simple concept, mis Abuelos were married. When I get married my husband will get that privilege, however I was not their wife, so neither one of them deserved the privilege of being catered to by me, yet I played the position very well.

Not even a year in, the true colors began to come out and the all too obvious signs began to pop up. I began collecting red flags as if they were roses, the bigger the bouquet the better. Can you hear a Dum dum diddy????? We were literally drinking 4-5 days a week, some days we had an awesome time but most days I became the dump. Here I was for the second time, allowing myself to be caught up in yet another situation ship. By year 3 I was tired of living this life of being intoxicated just to get through. Allowing myself to be treated less than I deserved. I decided I had enough and wanted out.

The decision was made, get him out, stop drinking again, get back to school, bust your tail working and focus on baby girl. You are better than this Janet!! It sounded so good! Then, yes of course, then my heart would kick in and I would really second guess myself. I knew I had fallen out of love an awfully long time ago, with myself and him. I was just going through the motions. I knew I needed time to regroup, I was suffocating, yet I guess it wasn't hurting bad enough, because after I told him I was done, I allowed him to stay. I continued to focus on me and baby girl, I began working crazy hours and began taking assignments where we wouldn't be together. In my mind I convinced myself that I allowed him to stay until he got on his feet. Yet by allowing him to stay in the house, I was sending a confusing message and the games began. The numbness to yet another heartbreak, I feel like I had wasted years again. I really had no energy for the games and my lack of interest, turned him into a different person.

A few months had passed, and life had gotten better for me. I was working for myself and an agency. Making great money, I was loving the freedom. This one particular night, I was getting myself together to head out to celebrate, with a few ladies from his family. I was dancing in the mirror, I looked damn good in my dress and shoes, I still wasn't drinking, had just smoked and I was absolutely feeling myself. I was ready to get out and celebrate the fact that I had just been accepted to nursing school.

"Where are you going and who are you going with?", he asked, staggering over his words. He knew what I was doing, he just sat himself in the living room until he had consumed enough liquid courage to approach me. I look at him sideways, "You don't have a right to question me, remember?"

He was pissed, you really could see the gates of hell in his eyes when his mood changed. However, he was met with a woman determined to get out that door, whether she had to fight her way out or not. He put his hands on me and I fought back hard. My beautiful hair got pulled out, my dress ripped, beer poured all over me and the rest of the time was a blur of events. The last thing I remember was the look of hate in his eyes, fighting to break free from the grip he had with both hands around my neck, trying to get air, the room spinning and a woman yelling, "Get off of her NOW!!!" I was so grateful his family showed up when they did, I may not have been here to write this story. I never did get out to celebrate the fact that I had been accepted to nursing school that night. However, I did get to celebrate something bigger, my gratitude for breathing right now and my freedom from yet another abusive situation, that I allowed to go on for quite too long.

"What's the matter honey?", my little old lady asked concerned. I kept my mind occupied by having long conversations with my patients. They were full of interesting stories, wisdom and knowledge. "Man problems?", she pushed a little further when I didn't respond to her quick enough. "No mama, its ME problems." I responded jokingly. "Well in that case, that's one that you can solve!" she answered sarcastically. "Every me problem is one you have created or allowed and those you have the power to change and solve. Right now, you not being genuinely happy is a me problem. Fix it. I like you better when you are happy. Pray for strength and faith, don't be afraid to ask your guardian angels for everything you want and believe it is yours.", she would always talk to me in a firm but loving tone. "Why my guardian angels though and not God?" I was curious. "Guardian angels, God, Allah, Buddha, Jehovah, Universe, whatever you choose to call it. It's all the same thing. We are spiritual beings that are all connected." She responded. That conversation triggered research and I began looking into everything she said. Spiritual beings? What did she mean by that? I had never stopped praying, and I realized I truly didn't believe what I was asking for, so I took her advice. I began writing letters to my dad again and asking him for everything I wanted. I wanted to pass nursing school, get a great paying job, oh and dad, don't forget the Cadillac Escalade. I really did carry a picture of my daughter and my Cadillac Escalade throughout the whole school year. It became a joke amongst the other students, girl you and this Cadillac Escalade, make sure you pick us up when you get it. We would all laugh, but I was serious as a heart attack, I was getting my dream truck.

That year in nursing school was hell. I was in school 5 days a week, enough homework to last the rest of the evening, eating whatever I picked up, taking care of my daughter, working double shift on the weekends. I was burning the candle at both ends so to speak. My diabetes said no, no sweetheart, we can't do this anymore.

It was almost the end of the year, and I was doing so good with holding onto my approved days. We only were allowed 5 approved days to take off the entire year. If we missed more than 5, we would not be allowed to graduate. I had felt the infection coming on in my mouth, my tooth was killing me. I was having a hard time concentrating and was swallowing Motrin like candy. I finally made an appointment with my doctor and got some antibiotics, hoping it would kill the infection and I could finish out the year then worry about my tooth. I woke up early the next day with my cheek swollen. I took my medicine and headed into clinicals. I was scheduled to be in the dialysis office, and I was really excited to see what it all included. I rushed into clinicals barely making it there on time, my face was throbbing, and I hadn't taken the time to look at my face since I showered that morning. The nurse that greeted us, took one look at my face, pulled me to the side and asked me was everything ok. I felt the tightness in my face, but I just responded, "Yes I'm ok, just a little tooth infection, I started my antibiotics already. I'll be ok." A look of concern came over her face, "I don't believe the antibiotics are working and I can't have you in here around my dialysis patients with any infection, even a little one. I think you need to go to the emergency room." I was so disappointed, thought ok I'll go the ER, they'll give me something else and back to school I go. Joke was on me.

By the time I reached the ER my face was looking like Professor Klump when the potion began to wear off. Yep, my whole side of my face was that big, lol. They ran my labs and realized I had a really bad infection that was spreading quickly. They began an aggressive IV antibiotic regimen and I had just won myself a nice little stay at the hospital. I got Friday off from school this week, I'll be here over the weekend and back to school on Monday. Remember MY plans, those were mine, I was still learning that my plans were irrelevant. The orthodontist, infection control and the endocrinologist all came to see me the next day. Their plans, start insulin shots in order to control my blood sugar levels, schedule me for oral surgery, in order to remove several damaged teeth at once that were the source of infection and at least 5 days of aggressive antibiotics after surgery.

"Oh, hell no doc, I'm not staying here that long, I have to get back to school. I am at the end of the year and if I miss more than 5 days I will not graduate. I got less than 30 days left. I have to graduate!" I was really irritated. "I understand, however if you wait 30 days, you won't be walking the stage, your classmates will be walking into your funeral. Now we will take the circumstances into consideration however I will not release you without knowing the infection is under control," he responded. I heard what he said but I wasn't listening, such a stubborn bull. My attitude was hurry up do what you gotta do and get me out of there.

Here comes the roller coaster of emotions again, here I was at the very end and now this. What is going on? Why am I being delayed from graduating? I don't get it. As the days passed, I began to lose hope.

I always had like this crazy indication that if I did what I was supposed to do in life, then life was just supposed to go smoothly. If I pray, go to church, write, do good for people, have faith and stay strong then naturally I would have what most call "a good life". My perspective was most definitely contorted. I was not exempt from life's curveballs, however a wise man by the name of Wayne Dyer once said, "By changing the way I looked at things, the things I looked at changed."

My oral surgeon did get me scheduled quickly for surgery. I was being poked and prodded several times a day, until they unfortunately blew out quite a few veins. They ended having to start a PICC line because my veins quit from all the antibiotics, fluids and daily blood draws. My fingers, belly and arms sore from blood sugar checks and insulin shots four times a day. It was exhausting to say the least. I was checking off the days after surgery and I knew my days were almost up. One great thing that kept me going was that my class was in that hospital for clinicals, and my friends were popping in all weeks to see me.

"Your levels have improved dramatically, however there is still cause for concern, we are going to have to keep you until Monday." The doctor said. "Doc I have one more day left to miss, and I won't graduate. If I am not released by Sunday in order to return to school Monday, I will sign myself out. This is my livelihood, and I won't throw this grueling year away. Plus, I can give myself my own IV antibiotics, just give me the stuff." I answered stubbornly. He began to giggle, "You are not yet licensed, and you cannot self-administer IV antibiotics. Now, I would advise you against leaving, but I will change your antibiotics and we will monitor your labs. Then we will see what we can do to get you out of here." I swear that doctor was so patient with me, the nurses were patient with me, my family was patient with me. I was not the easiest person to be around that week. I was determined to graduate nursing school.

"Dios hace todo por una razón. Pon lo en las manos de dios, ora por fortaleza, y nunca te olvide de tu fe." Abuela said. Once again, I heard her, but I wasn't listening. In those times I wasn't mature enough to take heed to the wisdom that was being passed to me. My thoughts were stuck in a depressive state, yet I hid it very well. "Si te oigo Abuela, pero porque siempre que biro la cabeza, ¿Dios me va metiendo un puno?" I asked, impatiently waiting for a clue. "Pues mi hija, las tormentas de vida siempre vienen, pero eres tú que tienes que hacer la decisión si vas a tener paciencia con dios para salir con nueva vida o si te vas a hogar en el agua." I loved my Abuela with every fiber of my being, when I did listen, I took away many golden nuggets that I pass onto my little reflections till this day.

(Translations: [33.] "God does everything for a reason. Put it in God's hands, pray for strength and never forget your faith." [34.] "Yes I hear you Grandma but how come every time I turn my head, God is throwing another punch?" [35.] "Well my daughter, the storms of life will always come, but it's up to you to decide whether you are going to have patience with God in order to come out with a new life or are you going to drown in the water?")

Later that night I decided to talk to my dad, before I went to sleep, I wrote him a long letter, this was my way of keeping him close. I remember asking him to please help me find strength to keep pushing, please put in a good word so that I can get out of here and graduate nursing school, please tell God to heal me so I can go home with my baby. Oh, and please don't forget that pretty Cadillac Escalade. I fell asleep with the beautiful memory of that smile on my dad's face when he seen his grandbaby bear Shadea walking on the sidewalk from that window.

I see his eyes light up then they quickly went dark, and he was laying back in the hospital bed fighting to breathe. I was screaming for the nurse, but it seemed as though, no one could hear me. He is gasping for air, why is no one helping him?! My dad turned my way, looked at me with his sunken eyes, struggling to breathe and put his hand out for me. I grabbed his hand, I was crying hysterically and telling him I loved him, as he closed his eyes and took his last breath.

I awakened sweating and, in a frenzy, I was ready to fight, was anxious, and just plain confused on where I was, I woke up to find out it was just a dream. Yet my dad allowed me to be there until the end this time, this was the way it was supposed to happen but what does this mean? Nonetheless I was restless until the sun came up. I struggled with whether to be happy he allowed me to be there with him until the end, even if it was a dream or was, he trying to tell me something else. For years I was so hard on myself simply for the factor that my dad died alone. As if I blame myself for not being there. Maybe it really wasn't meant for me to be there because just the dream alone was emotional and intense. Maybe that was his way of protecting me. My brain began those racing thoughts again. Hell no, not getting stuck here today, I got things to do.

I interrupted my thoughts by making the decision that I was going home. I covered my lines, took a shower, packed my stuff and by the time the nurse came with my meds, I was sitting up waiting, ready to sign my AMA papers and get out the door. I was graduating this year, if I rolled across the stage, in a wheelchair with IVs. Good practice for the student nurses, right? I started laughing at myself. I couldn't help but to turn my mood around with the silly, random thoughts that would pop in my head. It was the only way to keep my mind off the confusion of that dream and the anxiety of getting close to graduation.

"Please tell the doctor I am ready to go home, I need to graduate." I told her. "He knows Missy, you have been reminding him every day since you got here." She answered sarcastically. Shortly thereafter I was discharged to finish treatment on oral antibiotics, and I became a Betty Badass leaving that hospital. Huh? stop who from graduating? Shiiiiiittttt!! Not I, back to school I go tomorrow.

The determination to finish off the year strong was turned up about 5 more notches and that I did. The entire time I was struggling with newly adjusting to taking insulin and actually checking my blood sugar levels consistently yet I continued to persevere through the side effects and graduated.

After school ended, I went into beast mode. I was anxiously and impatiently waiting for the state to send me my date to sit for my testing. I got hired as a student nurse making less than I was making as a CNA, county job and quite an insult but I looked at it as a learning experience. I was given the opportunity to get experience as a nurse before I got licensed. However, I enjoyed the freedom of making my own schedule and money. Not to mention I couldn't pay for a Cadillac Escalade on that salary, lol.

Receiving my results while we were out on the Wildwood boardwalk celebrating my daughter's birthday, is a memory forever etched in my brain. I had told my family I had to move to a different section to get reception. I couldn't log in through my phone, so I called a friend of mine to get them for me. The results came back that I passed on my first-time testing. After all the sacrifice for this past year, I am now officially a Licensed Practical Nurse. I jumped all over the boardwalk crying, celebrating, dancing. It was so emotional; I couldn't believe it was over!!!

Every agency's dream employee, I most definitely was that person. You could literally call me at any time and if I wasn't working for someone else, I would come in for the right price. I was focused on having my dream car in one year from graduation. Back then, I was so loyal to an employer. I always took pride in the work I provided as a good-hearted person and good nurse. I treated my patients like family. I had to learn the hard way that these jobs could care less about their patients or me. I was a body to them, and those patients were instruments to make them money. I pushed the politics out of my head and just stayed focused on the goal, my dream truck parked in front of my house.

It took me less than a year and I achieved my goal. I remember the first person I went to see was my nursing teacher. It was a Saturday, and I went to her church, I found her in the worship hall and asked her to come outside. When she saw what was parked outside, she shrieked with excitement. A shiny black Cadillac Escalade parked in the lot. I had taken it off the picture and brought it into my reality.

I still couldn't believe my eyes every time I walked out the door. I am single mother, living in my own house, I am driving my dream truck, making great money with a great career. I was living the all-American dream. I had achieved what society has deemed as successful. Maybe this is what my dad was trying to tell me, the storm was coming to an end and new beginnings were in store. Humble yourself, then stop and cherish these moments.

"Humility is not thinking less of yourself, it's thinking of yourself less."

C.S. Lewis

Quick money, fast city life was always appealing to both me and my brother. We spent so much time in New York growing up as kids, it was as if we lived there. The same year I got my truck was the same year my little brother had gotten home from a 6-year bid in state prison for various crimes he had committed. From a liver transplant at 15 to a bid at 18, now being released at almost 24. He really was his father's child. I remember me and my cousin going together in the truck to pick him up at Riverfront in Camden NJ the day he was released. He was excited as hell to be going home after 6 years in style. I was happy as hell to have my little brother back home.

Our conversations on the way home, showed we had both grown up a lot over those years and I was at a point in life where I just wanted to work and chill with baby girl. I wanted to live a different life now. Yet, the excitement of the life always nagged at me, so it didn't take long for me to get snatched back up yet again. It was a battle similar to an addict, except we were addicted to a lifestyle. Trips up the road, parties galore, dating whoever I wanted and drinking like crazy yet again. Always surrounded by friends and family, money wasn't an issue, I was behind the scenes. I was living the good life, according to my standards, couldn't nobody bring me down. So quickly had I forgotten the message in that dream, humble yourself, stop and cherish these moments. Stop and what? I was going a 100 mph straight into a brick wall, with no safety gear, OKAY.

"Se están moviendo muy rápido. Cálmense, ante que dios te calme." Abuela said in her warning voice. "Yo no sé de lo que estás hablando Abuela, nosotros estamos calmado." Joey responded matter of factly. "Dios mío Papito, no me mientas, que bruta no soy. Yo no tengo que estar ahí para ver lo que están haciendo. Dios lo ve todo y el me lo ensena. Están los sueños que no me dejan dormir. A ti que to cogieron de preso otra vez y a ti que saliste en un accidente." Abuela snapped back. My heart dropped, as the years had passed my eyes were being opened up more and more to how gifted Abuela was, I became more aware to the events happening. So, when she spoke something inside of me would fear that it could happen, yet I would still carry on instead of just stopping and listening.

(Translations: [36]. "You are moving too fast. Calm down before God calms you down." [37]. I don't know what you're talking about Grandma, we are calm." [38]. "My God Papito, don't lie to me, because I'm not stupid. I don't have to be there to know what you two are doing. God sees everything and he shows it to me. These dreams won't allow me to sleep. You got arrested again and you had an accident."

"Regardless of how someone treated me, that doesn't mean I do the same to them. I do not become them because an eye for an eye only means I get more of what I don't want."

Janet M. Viera

Abuela's dreams never lied. My little brother ended getting hemmed up again. No question, he was coming right back home but I had to stomach him being gone again. All the running and partying took its toll on my body. Many of times I was parking at rest stops and just sleeping, because I was too tired to make it home. I started feeling nauseated and dizzy, my body was going through it. I missed my period which wasn't unusual considering the birth control. I mean the possibility was there, I was active, but my daughter was almost 11 years old, pregnancy was the last thing on my mind. I honestly believed I couldn't have any more children since I hadn't gotten pregnant all this time. I figured it was just my diabetes acting up from too much drinking and not enough sleeping. No worries, a trip to the doctor's office will get it straight, confirm its my diabetes, I'll get some sleep and keep it pushing through life.

Let's just say that trip to the doctor's turned my life right side up. What I didn't believe was possible, turned out to be 100% possible, I was pregnant. My oldest was now 11 years old, I was going to be starting all over. I was happy to know I could get pregnant, yet angry with myself for not being more careful. I wasn't in a relationship which meant once again I would be a single mom. Hard on myself was an understatement, I was just absolutely cruel to myself for allowing myself to get into a situation like this. I didn't believe in abortion so that was out of the question, what other choice did I have but to buckle up buttercup and handle life.

Shortly after finding out, I received a phone call I wish I would've never answered. I was on my way back from up the road and against my intuition that was screaming, "girl get to your mom's house and go to sleep, don't waste your time," I decided to go anyway. The discomfort and anxiety I felt, gave me goosebumps. I wanted to get the awkward conversation done and over with, I had no time for feelings or relationships. After all was said and done, I realized how cold I allowed life to make my heart or maybe it was just the suck it buttercup attitude. Either way I knew it wasn't cool to treat others as they have treated me. Yet when you're moving too fast, you learn how to just out on a mask and move on in life.

That ride to my mom's house seemed so long, I was lost in deep thought, and the last thing I remember was feeling dizzy and right before I passed out, I was headed for a tree. I woke up with white smoke all around. I immediately cried out when I realized what had happened, I was bleeding but grateful to be alive. I managed to fight my way out of the truck. I don't even remember how the police, and everyone got there. I remember that every section of my shiny black Cadillac Escalade was crushed flat by the electrical pole I took up from the ground and ending up in the woods. The only part that wasn't crushed, was where I was sitting on the driver's side. I was rushed to the hospital to check on my baby. Thank goodness she was ok too. From the looks of that truck, I knew Abuela prayers definitely brought my guardian angels out to protect me that night. To see that the only section that was intact was where I was sitting, I was in shock.

The games I played with my own mind were surreal. This was your karma, you shouldn't have been such a winch, that's what you get. Although I was incredibly grateful for being alive, I had led myself to believe that the meeting is why the accident occurred. Maybe if you wouldn't have gone you would still have your truck, ole bad luck charm. Go ahead, have a good laugh, I do now. To believe that this occurred because of someone else was immature, because I had to face the cold hard facts. No Janet this happened because your tail was moving too fast, and even though God sent you the warning through your Abuela you didn't slow down, so he stopped you!!

I calmed down really quick after that, who wouldn't after you get a second chance at life. I made minimal moves, focused on work and on having a healthy baby. Tatyana was my first pregnancy since being diagnosed with diabetes. The lack of sleep played heavy on my blood sugar levels, which in turned messed with my mental bad. I couldn't eat what I wanted, I had to be mindful of everything or else she could end up with diabetes, pretty tough with pregnancy cravings.

After 12 years of being an only child I was concerned on how Shadea was going to react. She was so excited to be a big sister and I was so grateful she was accepting her role gracefully. By 8 months Tatyana was estimated to be 13lbs and breech, I was scheduled for my c-section before month 9, any longer in the oven and she would've been 20lbs, lol. I decided to allow Shadea in the operating room with me to witness the birth of her baby sister. Baby girl Tatyana was born a healthy 10lbs.

As for me, starting all over was extremely difficult, from a kid who is independent, to diaper bags and car seats. I was going through it. I felt small for once again getting pregnant out of wedlock and disappointing my grandparents. Then working, taking care of 2 girls, and still trying to be young was not a good combo at all. I lost myself again and I was desperate to get her back.

Chapter: 9

"MOM SHE DROWNED!!", HEARING THE FEAR IN MY OLDEST DAUGHTER'S VOICE, WILL BE ETCHED IN MY SOUL. IT WAS AN OPEN WOUND THAT HAS NOW HEALED, HOWEVER THE SCAR WILL ALWAYS BE THERE AS A REMINDER OF THE DAY THAT CHANGED MY LIFE FOREVER. MY AWAKENING, I WAS NEVER THE SAME PERSON AGAIN.

"MOM SHE DROWNED!!", hearing the fear in my oldest daughter's voice, will be etched in my soul. It was an open wound that has now healed; however, the scar will always be there as a reminder of the day that changed my life forever. My awakening, I was never the same person again.

On the early morning of February 14, 2008, I went to the ER with pain and bleeding. After hours of testing, I was discharged and told to prepare myself for a miscarriage. Just finding out I was pregnant and hearing that horrible word, I left the hospital with a heavy heart, tears in my eyes and my mind in a cloud as I went on about my day. All I could do was pray, God if it's your will then please have your way. Being pregnant again when my Tatyana was only 11 months old was the last thing I needed.

We are all human; I say this not to take away from the wrong decision I made but more so to soften the blow to myself. The shame, and guilt, I have had to process, trumps any shame thrown my way by others. I made a terrible decision to run down the street to the store leaving my oldest daughter to watch my baby girl. As the thoughts of possibly losing my unborn child weighed heavily on my mind I get the most dreading phone call, my oldest daughter, screaming, crying repeating over and over, "Mom she drowned!!!"

My heart once again dropped as I stomped my heavy foot to the gas racing to get home. I arrive to see flashing lights in my front yard, a mother's worst nightmare, I wouldn't wish that feeling on anyone. I ran through my door to see a police officer working on my baby girl who was purple. I heard my baby girl trying to cry but only being able to whine. I was only able to hold and comfort her for a split second before the medics ran through my door, taking her from my arms to get her to the ER. Although she was breathing the danger was far from over and she was transferred to Children's

Hospital of Philadelphia or as we know it CHOP. She was kept overnight for observation to be sure that she had no adverse effects from the near drowning accident. All throughout the night I barely slept. I see her little body jumping in her sleep, as well as hearing her whine sporadically through the night. It tore me apart to think she could be having nightmares from this and in that moment, I felt like my girls were better off without me.

That night I had to call out from one of my jobs, due to being in the hospital with my daughter. The next morning, I received a call from my Director of Nurses telling me not to come back to work. She was under the impression that I called out because I requested that day off and got denied. She was sadly mistaken, and even after showing her paperwork, she wouldn't even consider righting her wrongs. I became bitter with employers, I realized I was only good to them for as long as I allowed myself to be used. Although it hurt financially, I personally took it as a sign that I needed to spend more time with my baby girls and less time away at work, it's a shame it took almost losing my baby girl for me to see that it wasn't worth sacrificing my time, attention, and love, for a dollar.

That evening the doctors came in, said she had passed all testing and was cleared to go home. They reminded me of how grateful as most kids don't survive without adverse effects. They informed me on signs to look out for and to bring her back immediately if she shows these signs. They never mentioned the emotional toll it would take on her and our family.

My intention when I got her home was to bathe her immediately, since she had been at the hospital overnight. I quickly was brought back down to reality when I took her into bathroom. She held onto me so tight and wouldn't let go. I sat in that bathroom in tears, just holding that little girl, apologizing over and over All I could think was the fear my oldest daughter must have felt in finding her little sister, unresponsive, under the water in that bathtub. And the fear Tatyana must have felt as she was losing her breath. I held onto that little girl like she was me, feeling the fear and abandonment of both of my girls, that mommy wasn't there when they needed her. I felt like the world's most horrible mother, and I needed to find a way for my daughter to see that she was her little sister's hero. Shadea immediately acted when she found her sister, had she not, the ending to this story would have been hugely different.

It wasn't but a few weeks after when I was contacted by the chief of police. He came to my home and stated that they were under the impression that Shadea was a teenage mom, and they had no clue she wasn't the mom. The press got a hold of the story, they wanted to do a front cover story for their paper on the young girl who saved her sister. Could they release my information? I looked at this as great news, a chance to show Shadea she was her little sister's hero. I agreed to do the story. They came to our home and I was completely blindsided by how media worked. The news is supposed to tell the truth right? No, the news is supposed to sell stories and that is exactly what they did.

That story hit the paper and my phone did not stop ringing, news stations showed up at our door wanting to interview us. Relatives and foes looking for gossip, it was bad enough I tortured myself but now I had the rest of the public making judgements on me "not being here more for my kids", not knowing the whole story. Just taking what the news had chopped and edited as the truth. Only one newscaster from CBS 6 news reported a completely honest story and I will forever be grateful for her.

The aftermath was overwhelming. Sarcastic comments when someone would recognize me in the store. I didn't much care what people had thought of me up until this point. However they were attacking my motherhood, and what I thought would be a great way to show Shadea she was her sister's hero, turned out to be quite the opposite for me. I didn't know then that I was simply reflecting what I felt within myself through other people. So the desire to leave the small town mentality began to resurface again. It was really my desire to run from the pain, shame and guilt. Instead of facing it head on.

Fast forward, my son decided he was not going anywhere and months later he was born in October, a healthy 8lbs 9oz. What would've been a joyous time for most, was extremely depressing for me. I was once again a single mom to now 3 children, with no one but my grandparents to help. I'll blame that on my bad choices only. My biggest struggle, was not feeling like I was worthy of being blessed to be these angels mother. Why would he keep picking me?

"And when great souls die, after a period peace blooms, slowly and always irregularly. Spaces fill with a kind of soothing electric vibration. Our senses restored, never to be the same, whisper to us. They existed, they existed. We can be, Be and be better for they existed."

Maya Angelou

It wasn't but a few weeks after when I was contacted by the chief of police. He came to my home and stated that they were under the impression that Shadea was a teenage mom, and they had no clue she wasn't the mom. The press got a hold of the story, they wanted to do a front cover story for their paper on the young girl who saved her sister. Could they release my information? I looked at this as great news, a chance to show Shadea she was her little sister's hero. I agreed to do the story. They came to our home, and I was completely blindsided by how media worked. The news is supposed to tell the truth, right? No, the news is supposed to sell stories and that is exactly what they did.

That story hit the paper and my phone did not stop ringing, news stations showed up at our door wanting to interview us. Relatives and foes looking for gossip, it was bad enough I tortured myself but now I had the rest of the public making judgements on me "not being here more for my kids", not knowing the whole story. Just taking what the news had chopped and edited as the truth. Only one newscaster from CBS 6 news reported a completely honest story and I will forever be grateful for her.

The aftermath was overwhelming. Sarcastic comments when someone would recognize me in the store. I didn't much care what people had thought of me up until this point. However, they were attacking my motherhood, and what I thought would be a great way to show Shadea she was her sister's hero, turned out to be quite the opposite for me. I didn't know then that I was simply reflecting what I felt within myself through other people. So, the desire to leave the small-town mentality began to resurface again. It was really my desire to run from the pain, shame and guilt. Instead of facing it head on.

Fast forward, my son decided he was not going anywhere and months later he was born in October, a healthy 8lbs 9oz. What would've been a joyous time for most, was extremely depressing for me. I was once again a single mom to now 3 children, with no one but my grandparents to help. I'll blame that on my bad choices only. My biggest struggle was not feeling like I was worthy of being blessed to be these angel's mother. Why would he keep picking me?

"*Love is what we are born with, Fear is what we learn, the spiritual journey is the unlearning of fear and the acceptance of love back in our hearts.*"

Marianne Williamson

Once again, I began picking up private cases, I enjoyed the freedom of making money on my own. I still worked for an agency here and there, but the hustler mentality was in my blood since young, I was just trying to figure out ways to capitalize the right way and be home with my babies more. Shadea was growing up into a young lady in front of my eyes.

Very few people knew I struggled with mental health; I did a great job of covering it up. I was raised to believe you handled your mental health at home and that may have worked for me at that time, but it wasn't working for Shadea. She acted out in different ways, and I knew in my heart these were cries for help. I knew all she wanted was me, but I didn't even know where me had disappeared to. I would stand in the mirror and couldn't recognize the person staring back at me most days.

We got Shadea the help and I even halfhearted tried some counseling sessions myself, but being consistent with trusting someone with my emotions, absolutely could not get there. I had such a sad indication that in order to speak about my emotions, I would have to trust you, in order to trust you, I would have to care about you and it seemed as though everyone I have cared about enough to share my emotions with has either left or died, so in order to protect myself from feeling the pain of abandonment, I would shut my emotions off to anyone outside my pen and journal. Learning to open my heart back up to love was a journey in itself.

"Love is what we are born with, Fear is what we learn, the spiritual journey is the unlearning of fear and the acceptance of love back in our hearts."

Marianne Williamson

After RaSean came I barely had time to breath, let alone worry about my mental health. I had my hands full with that boy and I swear, God knew what he was doing by making him the last. Had that boy came first, he would have been an only child. I am for sure that I would have performed the tubal myself. I really thought Abuela had limitless patience when it came to kids, RaSean broke that, lol. He was crawling by 4-5 months, walking by 9 months, running by a year old and potty trained by a year and a half. Terrible twos? Those didn't exist because he started at one when he did a magic trick, escaping his car seat, then jumping in my front seat and attempting to drive off with my car. As you can see history repeats itself through our children (insert sarcasm here, lol). Did they ever end you ask? Not quite sure as I have still have a 12 year old who yells at the top of his lungs randomly, scaring the crap out of me. So, it's safe to say I still have my hands full.

If you ask God for a break, he'll give it you. However, it won't be on your time nor your way. Going out to poetry shows, open mics, being in studios for hours on end became the new norm. I grew a new love performing spoken word. Writing pieces, performing pieces, meeting new people, traveling to new states and venues. Discovering new creativities within myself. I felt so alive behind a microphone. It became my release and my saving grace.

The beautiful friendships I created through this period in my life will always be special in my heart. One in particular, whom will always be special is the individual who brought the reality to me about my stage name. He proceeds to tell me that I should consider changing my stage name from Mentally Imprisoned. I asked him, "Why? I like that name and plus that's how I feel. Like I have all these things just jumbled up in my head and I want people to know I am setting myself free through my poetry." He replies,

"Have you ever considered that your words become you? How free do you plan on being free if continue to call yourself that name?" Turned around my whole view, drove all the way home, in search of a new stage name that points me in the right direction of my authentic message.

Becoming a mom early at 16, then almost 12 years becoming a mom again, on top of working and still trying to find time for me definitely had its challenges.

Things weren't like before; Shy didn't know then her mother was fighting an internal battle not to fall victim to her past. A major life change was well overdue. I had already experienced the good life, the street life and the successful life, now I was looking to experience the simple life. I needed a new environment away from the people, places and things that influenced any chance of me returning to someone I no longer was anymore.

Spending time with my immediate family became even more important as I played with the idea of leaving far away from my hometown. I began having deeper conversations with my pops and my grandparents. I realized their wisdom is what helped keep me grounded. I was flying off the handle less and less as I began to learn how to discipline my anger. I was living in a fog so much that I never took notice that the same exact hurt I put out in my past, was the same hurt that was returning to me in the present. It was as if Valentine's Day 2008 cleared the fog and woke me up with so many questions that I needed answers to. I had woken up to the fact that nothing was more important than the love for myself and my children.

Years would pass, as I would talk about leaving and no one would believe me. I'm out of here next month, next month would come and I'm still here. I struggled with leaving my grandparents behind. The heart-to-heart conversations are what helped me decide to leave everything I have ever known and step out in faith.

MY POPS ROB AND THE GRANDBABIES IN 2011

This one particular conversation was extremely special, because up until now I would talk about the events in general, but I had never fully opened up to anyone about Valentine's Day 2008. It happened in March 2012; we had just finished celebrating Tatyana's birthday with the family. After everyone left, I went to the back room with my pops for a session. Out of the blue he asks, "How come you have never been right since you and that man broke up? I know what it's like to be in love, but damn mother f**ker, you just aren't the same anymore." I choked, started laughing and coughing, "Pops is that really what y'all believe?" I managed to get that out through the laughter. "Pops I haven't been the same since I got the news I was due to miscarry, I haven't been the same since hearing the fear in my daughter's voice when she called me that night, I haven't been the same since I held my baby girl in my arms purple, I haven't been the same since losing my job because I chose my daughter, I haven't been the same since I been carrying all this shame and guilt for leaving that night, I haven't been the same since being judged by so many for my errors, as if they didn't have any. Pops I haven't been the same since February 14, 2008, and I will never be the same again. No one else had anything to do with this change, it's strictly a personal battle." It was a huge release to get those words out. He sat there with me for close to 2 hours pouring wisdom and knowledge into me. I left the house that night feeling so grateful for Pops being placed in our lives when my dad was taken away. Feeling so grateful for time with family, feeling so grateful for my kids, my grandparents, feeling grateful for life period.

"My fear of abandonment had influenced just about every decision I had made up until this point in life. It was as if I trained myself not to love people or things too deeply, simply because they were going to leave or die anyway."

"Rob tuvo un accidente, tienes que ir al hospital ahora," Abuela said. I tried calling everyone I could to find out what happened and was just told to go to the hospital. I was escorted to a small room where my family was waiting, my mom's face soaked in tears, the feeling of my heart dropping to my stomach was all too familiar, I prepared myself for what I already knew I was going to hear. My pops had a heart attack, a mile from home. He had just dropped off RaSean to my mom because he was headed to an appointment and one mile from home, he had a heart attack while driving.

Most barely survived the death of one dad and now I was being forced to survive, two in one lifetime? God are you serious right now? What a helluva curve ball there! All I kept repeating in my head was, my dude you left us too? Now who are we supposed to turn to?

At one point in my life, every time something made me feel really good or a blessing came, it's like I would brace myself for the devastating news that was to follow. This was one of my flaws. I found it difficult to enjoy the warm and fuzzy feelings for too long due to not knowing how to discipline my feelings and thoughts.

My old dear friend, alcohol came back to visit, spent just about the whole time tipsy. The thought of having to shut a box on the face of yet another loved one, was just too much reality to face, so I definitely guzzled a few shots before the service, "Do what you have to do and F**K what people think!" is what my Pops would've said and that's exactly what I'm going to do. Had I known then what I know now.

It's easier said than done when years of compounded unhealed grief became a snowball effect in my life. Destroying everything it came in contact with on my path. I had been partying pretty hard for a few months after Pops passed, looking at the pain in my mom's face as she tried to push through the hurt, was reason enough for me. Forgetting that I was also escaping my pain only for the moment. So many who were taken away too soon. Could I trust anyone not to leave?

ACCOUNTABILITY

Accountability is a mature thing to do... Taking accountability for whatever it is you don't agree with that is occurring in your own life, taking accountability for your own problems, taking accountability for things you have created with your own thoughts, choices, or decisions.... past, present, or future. Whenever I come across hurdles in life, I take accountability. I choose to respond and ask myself what could I have done differently? Did I bring a different energy? Did I say something in a hurtful way? And the list goes on... Meaning I go home, look MYSELF in the mirror and ask me all types of questions, first! Then I come to terms with the facts that hurt people, hurt people. And you realize that some find comfort in their complacency to point the finger at everyone but themselves, and you accept the fact, that it's truly personal. I cannot take anyone else's feelings to heart; those emotions are not mine to carry. Unfortunately, emotional maturity is not something that is practiced widely across the board, you personally cannot change those facts. However, when you look at things from a different perspective you begin to have more compassion and kindness for individuals who come across your path, whether you agree with them or not, because each one is a reflection. Whether it's a lesson that still needed to be learned from the past, a mission that needed to be completed in the present, or the tools you needed to break generational curses for the future, each one played a role. You cannot control how others may have hurt you, you cannot control how others may have abandoned you, you cannot control events that may have occurred in your life. What you can control is whether you choose to respond or react. Take accountability for your part. I have been choosing to respond with unconditional love, and forgiveness because that is what serves me best. Having animosity, anger, resentment, regret in my heart towards others is too heavy a burden to carry. Accountability is about doing what's right, period....

Chapter 10

"Vulnerability is a wave, surf it, go with flow, the more you practice it, the more you heal your soul."

Janet M. Viera

Depression, anxiety, isolation and grief. Basically, that snowball came rolling down that mountain fast as hell. Getting drunk more often than I care to admit. I decided to take a night away, to go and enjoy myself at the Puerto Rican Day Parade. As I was leaving to head out to NY, that voice said, "Stay home Janet." Yet I chose not to listen, AGAIN.

Stitching

Que Bonita Bandera,

Such a beautiful flag,

Que Bonita Bandera,

Such a beautiful flag,

Que Bonita Bandera,

La bandera puertorriqueña,

Red... White... Blue....

She was not describing America, she was talking about dancing on Fifth Ave,

Red,

She bled our pride from the shore to the streets,

White,

The bones and flesh that changed our fate,

Blue,

From under one sky,

One God we lived and loved in the second weekend in June,

To celebrate,

Our Nuyorican Pride.

She wants to be back out so bad inside,

Dancing merengue, salsa and adding a twist to the bachata with a slide,

Waving her flag with pride yelling,

"Yo soy Boricua!!" and having the crowd answer,

"Pa que tú lo sepa!!!"

"Weeeeppppaaaa!!" enjoying life and smiling as she dances away,

Instead, she is sitting in his back seat,

With a feeling of defeat overcoming her.

She is sensing how he's feeling so bold,

Taking her down unknown roads,

It's 90 degrees outside, yet she's freezing below,

As she feels her sweats being snatched down to her ankles,

He was as yellow as the cab he drove,

In her eyes, cowardly, treacherous, gutless, and deceitful,

The product of a damaged soul,

"Where is your Boricua pride now?" he yelled.

And with each pound she would lose herself in the sound of the congos,

Where she was just 10 hours ago.

Lost in the parade.

Consuming and savoring each nutcracker that would come her way,

Eating pinchos,

Flags swaying,

The guitarist playing those strings so forceful,

As everyone unites in singing the national anthem,

"La tierra de él Borinquén donde nacido yo, es jardín muy lindo del mágico primor."

Maybe just maybe, if she reminisces over this memory enough in her head,

It will take her mind off this cold steel barrel that could her to bed permanently,

Although he's already left her for dead,

Molesting her intelligence,

Corrupting her confidence,

Snatching her dignity,

The only fight she has lost in her life.

She's now petrified,

To the point where she no longer wants to be seen by the public eye,

Having the hardest time,

Rebuilding a flag, she once had so much pride in,

As she hears him in everything,

A flag she once looked at with so much love in her eyes, she now cuts to pieces,

As it is a constant reminder of,

"Where is your Boricua pride now???"

As the time goes on, she realizes, she has to get to stitching.

Primarily because she's too bull headed to just let him win,

She just won't let him win,

She can't let him win,

She has to get this process started, by stitching,

Taking each red, white and blue piece and stitching,

Gaining her strength, confidence, and self-esteem through stitching,

Learning humility and forgiving in stitching.

Gaining pride in a place she'd thought she'd never see it again,

Her Flag,

For with her pride and her beautiful smile, she will leave a trace of peace, love and blessings,

In each town, city or suburb she steps in,

For she has overcome her fear through stitching.

Janet M. Viera

It isn't too difficult to figure what occurred on that night. Just one of those events I have chosen to block out most of it for my sanity. This poem was my release.

After this night, I turned ALL the way down. I felt like God had hit me in the head enough. I was stubborn and most definitely suffered the consequences because of my stubbornness. Pieces of my soul had been snatched out of my body and I was a shell.

Literally would sit in my room as people would come knocking on the door. I wouldn't even acknowledge it. My whole focus was trying to make sure my mom was ok. I was reaching out more and more to check on her, I could literally feel her pain, it was unexplainable and quite frankly weird to me at that time, but I knew I had to figure out a way to see what exactly was happening. Big changes were under way, and I was drained of energy for simply existing. I could not continue to live this way.

Where do I begin though? Who could point me in the right direction? The craziest part about it, it was my mom. I began to notice that mom had cut out the drinking and had begun going to church every week. I began seeing her reading her bible and it encouraged me to pick mines back up. Seeking this comfort and peace we all were searching for.

In the same chapter, the word empathic came across my path and I really began to do more research on empaths. I was curious to know how to clear my path. I came across authors like Napoleon Hill, Wayne Dyer, Abraham Hicks and the list goes on. I became interested in learning more about truly achieving a sense a peace. I wanted to experience that genuine happiness wholeheartedly and consistently. I now had three little people who depended on me. So, this roller coaster within my mind and heart really had to be stopped.

Engulfing myself in self-development books, I opened a doorway to a portal in my mind. I read of other's stories of how they triumphed through times just like my life and it turned my whole perspective around.

This time when I made the decision to get out of NJ, I told nobody until it was almost time for me to leave. I had learned that the minute you told people of your plans, most would try to talk you out of it because of their own fears. So, I decided on leaving after my oldest daughter graduated high school.

Not even a week after she graduated 2013, I packed up what I could fit in my truck and off we went 1500 miles away from home to Dallas, Texas. Shadea made it through about a month and she wanted out of the Texas life quickly. As for myself the excitement of a brand-new place caught my attention quickly and my decision to stay was solid. I was ready to build a whole new life with me and my children.

So many plans were made, once again MY plans, those don't seem to work out too well when God's plans are different. Hard head makes a soft behind, because my plans didn't work out and about a month after arriving in Dallas, I ended up sleeping in my truck in a Walmart parking lot with 2 small children and most of our belongings. I remember walking through the Walmart and feeding my kids what I could, simply because of my pride. I remember feeling at the lowest of the lows. My pride got in the way of reaching out to anyone for help, for fear of being rejected. Yet, everyone calling me trying to find out what's going on and trying to convince me to come back home. I refused to answer, the only one I wanted to talk to was my daughter. Thoughts of leaving this earth crossed my mind more times than I care to admit, however knowing my kids would have no one is what stopped me. I was at the bottom of the barrel with no way out in sight.

God answered my prayers in astonishing ways. We met some truly kind strangers who allowed me and my children to stay in their home until we found a shelter to relocate to. Even went as far as giving up their bed, simply so we could sleep comfortably. Introduced us to their church, who then became our first church family in Texas. Baaaabbbyyy they showed us that good ole small town, down south hospitality. I will cherish and forever be grateful for every last one of those beautiful souls. They have become family and we still keep in touch.

Spent my days searching for places to stay, visited so many different shelters trying to find a place for us to sleep. Some places were so scary, I cried taking the tours. It was one particular place I walked into, and it looked like a prison, the "you are a burden" vibe was heavy. For simply asking a question you caught attitude, I was floored. This was something straight out of a movie.

Placing a disclaimer is the only way to satisfy your curiosity. Yes I had the option to go back home to NJ, if I chose to. However, I chose to listen to my intuition instead that kept urging me to stay in TX, read on to find out why.

It was not long before I found a women's shelter that would take me and my kids. It was a decent place that was not overcrowded, so we were blessed to receive a separate room and bathroom. We even received a cute little key card, helping me in creating a story for my kids that we were staying in a hotel. Once the key card unlocked the door and you entered the room, it was a different story for me. I closed my eyes prayed and convinced myself this was only temporary. I was grateful for a roof over our heads, food in our stomachs, we are blessed.

Room at women's shelter.

They had activities for the kids, they were meeting friends, I was meeting new people, we really were filled with every hope upon coming there. We were encouraged to have family dinners together and everyone had a part in upkeeping all areas. It was a system that worked for the most part.

No phones or technology were allowed in the building, however that is how I kept my sanity, so I got them in however I could. You were mandated to attend church services every single night, even if you had a church home. At first, I really did not mind it, I was seeking God in every aspect. So, the more praise, worship, and prayer, the happier I was. At this point in my journey, I had spent 75% of my life attending Pentecostals churches and events. Along with a few other I opened myself to learning about. This place here was over the board, lol. Due to the fact the services were based on volunteers, we received messages from all different perspectives of religion. Being the Curious George I am, naturally I began to ask all kinds of questions, whenever something was said Some were received well, others were not received well at all. It was mini discipleship boot camp, and I had no intention of joining their one-year long women's cult. I was so grateful to have my small little church family, even if it was just on Sundays.

Reading, music and poetry were my escapes. Reading, meditating and journaling about my bible became consistent. I felt like messages were coming to me on a consistent basis. My mind would be thinking about different things, here is a message to clarify it. I began to focus on seeing the signs I was being sent of which direction to go.

It was not long before all the rules got to me, it seemed as though they were made up as they went. Work was not coming as quickly so because I couldn't find an opportunity, I created one. I had achieved obtaining a contract for a private duty case. I had to sign it and fax it back, in order to lock in the deal and get the first month deposit. I went into the main office simply asking to use the fax machine for hiring. I was told no; I would have to find the nearest staples and fax it from there. I did not understand why faxing a document for a contract for work was such a big deal, but I was told later what the deal was and to be prepared, things were about to turn. I began getting a lot of the heavier jobs in the house until one day I was outside at break time and this older woman approached me. She gave me a list of places to look into, informed me to get moving because once you tell these people no to their yearlong program, they begin to make it extremely uncomfortable for you to stay here.

I got the contract and was scheduled to start work in a few days. I had become cool with a few of the moms in there and they would help me out with babysitting since I was working nights. Social worker found out and put a stop to it immediately. I was just trying to figure out ways to make it in a strange place, with two small children and now instead of helping, you were attempting to stop my livelihood. You do not mess with 3 things, my God, my family, and my money. I was still struggling with my anger, and I cussed her out, bad.

In the meanwhile, I had taken the woman's advice and begun looking into another place to stay. Within 2 weeks I received a call back for an interview to a more organized program. I could save my money and actually work towards getting into my own place, which was the goal right? I prayed on it every day until my interview. I was getting out of here come hell or high water. Wasn't going to have me dressed like a nun singing Kumbaya somewhere, no sorry bob, lol.

Interview day came and I went in there like our lives depended on it, because it did. So many questions on what my goals were, and I answered each question genuinely. I told her a little bit of my story and how I was determined to build this great life for my children. When we finished the interview and she crushed my heart when she told me she was extremely impressed with my interview, however there is at least a 2-month waiting list to get into a room. I had made it on the waiting list; however, I knew I didn't have 2 months to stay at this other place. I left the interview and began to pray again. I had come to another crossroad; I had no control of the outcome, and my anxiety began to kick in again..

"Stand up straight and realize who you are, that you tower over your circumstances. You are a child of God, stand up straight!!"

Maya Angelou

Not calling home became consistent, I didn't want to hear the lectures, or the gossip so I wouldn't call. My family couldn't understand that I know I could come back home but I wasn't doing this for them, I was doing this for me and my kids. It would hurt to hear my Abuela's voice, as she would attempt to encourage me, yet also try to convince me to come back home. That stubborn bull wasn't backing down. I knew deep in my heart; I came to TX for a purpose, and I wasn't leaving until it was fulfilled. God was going to tell me when it was time to move on and   so many people began to drop off like flies, so many were truly upset that I was choosing this path. It wasn't for them to understand my journey. It was for me to experience it and overcome it.

"¿Y si me enfermo, quien me va a cuidar Janetcita?" she would always ask me. "Abuela si te enfermas, eso será lo único que me trae de vuelta a Nueva Jersey. Les prometo que volveré a cuidar de los dos. ¿Si no te vienes a vivir conmigo primero?" I answered giggling. I knew it was a long shot, but I dang sure tried as well. They had lived in this house for 30+ years at this point, getting her to move to TX was a nice thought, but I knew it wasn't happening.

However, this particular day, I called to speak with my Abuelo. I was seeking his humbleness and biblical counsel. His ability to help me see the lessons in what I experienced or read was unmatched. I explained to him what had occurred with my situation, the interview, the new place. I wanted to know what God's next steps were with me. Hello Abuelo tap into your golden source, aren't you on a first name basis with this dude? "Pues hija, lo puedo llamar a ver si me contesta, pero él siempre está ocupado con las oraciones de nosotros. Papa Dios, Janetcita quiere que le dé el plan que tiene. ¿Se lo vas a dice o no? No sé, no oigo nada mi hija." Laughter is what held our family together through some pretty tough times. That evening we laughed and cried, as he once again reminded me of having patience through these times to wait on God's answer. Pray, then let go and let God. My Abuelo was humble yet powerful man, divinely guided and blessed with the gift of speaking life into you. When he delivered a message, you felt it in your soul. When he laid hands on you to pray, you felt it through every nerve in your body. Many people said I had the same effect on them, as I would read my poetry.

Abuelo was proud to be having conversations like this with me. He prayed for many years for us to come to know God and seek his counsel. I knew he wasn't happy with my current situation; however, my grandfather was the only one who didn't attempt to talk me into coming back. He knew the struggle of leaving the streets behind, moving in a more spiritual way, making real connections and learning this more peaceful way of living. No longer did I want to live my life looking over my shoulder. He already been through the process of shedding his layers of the cocoon and becoming the butterfly. He was just patiently waiting for us to be awakened. Abuelo rarely publicly got upset and I wanted to learn his secret. We ended that beautiful and emotional conversation with prayers from both of them together. I fell asleep crying that night, "God I have no idea where you are taking my story but please just take the pen. My trust is in you."

Boy that Viera and Taurus stubbornness combined (insert eye roll here, lol) I would allow God to take my pen to continue writing my story, then the minute he wrote a line I didn't like, I was snatching that Pilot G2 Pro right back. I know my guardian angels threw quite a few chancletas at my head.

163

They even pulled out the Mr. Act Right Belt a few times. They were about sick of me, lol.

(Translations: [39.] "And if I get sick, who is going to take care of me Janecita?" [40.] "Grandma you getting sick will be the only thing bringing me back to NJ. I promise I will be back to take care of you both. If you don't come to live with me first?"

Abuelo and Abuelas prayers are always working though. It took about another two weeks, and I received a call from the family shelter. Unexpectedly, a family moved into their own place and a room had opened up for us to move in. I didn't believe in coincidences, so that wasn't unexpectedly, that room opened up for us. I was in awe at how fast he moved when you prayed boldly and had their consistent daily prayer of protection surrounding you. November 2013 the room will be ready for us, and I couldn't be happier. I was grateful for having a roof over our head. However, I was truly looking forward to being treated like a human being again.

Packed my stuff in my truck and only kept a book bag in the room, with enough clothes and hygiene for the day. Word began to get around the building that I had gotten into that program and before I knew it jealousy began to flare. Completely oblivious to the fact that a lot of those same mothers were on the waiting list for that program, and I was chosen ahead of them. I had nothing to do with that super move, it was all God's work and my grandparents' prayers.

"Walking into their new room, I cried. This was a blessing I was looking forward to showing my kids."

When I finally got the call and the opportunity to move in, I was out of the other building before I could hang up the phone. I knew where I was, Texas, and not a soul could convince me to drink the Kool aid in that building, ok.

Walking into their new room, I cried. This was a blessing; I was looking forward to showing my kids. It may not seem like much, however after sleeping, cramp up in a truck with our stuff, this was heaven. A new hope for us.

Observant and quiet, people began to talk, I didn't come off as friendly. It wasn't like I was going up to people and introducing myself. I was laser focused on my children, getting more cases and getting the hell into my own place. I had no extra time to be friendly, and I was still missing the lesson in this situation. Trust the process.

Working like a single mother trying to get her kids in a house, I ran through that program in record time. Within a month I was financially in position to move into my own place. I began looking and was approved for a townhouse in North Dallas. Finished up the classes in December and was hoping to be in my place by Christmas but unfortunately God said not yet. Getting my place was more important so unfortunately, I was unable to travel back home for the holidays. My kids were abundantly blessed with their room filled to top with gifts however we were one of three families who had to stayed behind because we had nowhere to go, while everyone else was out with their family on weekend passes. The other 2 families didn't celebrate Christmas, so it was me and my kids, under the Christmas tree alone. I had to keep telling them I was crying happy tears, but in reality, I was missing the hell out of my daughter and family. We spent the rest of the day outside, exploring all downtown. Despite what we were going through at the moment we made so many memories and made the best of the rest of our day.

By January 10th of 2014 I was moving into our townhouse. I had nothing but twin beds, one couch a table, a set of pots and pans, and our clothes. I didn't care, we were Home. It didn't take us long to unpack. We were so happy, and I was feeling blessed. Little by little I got my house in order.

It didn't take but seven days and I was hit with another storm. "They shot him Sis!! Over some BS!! A f***king punk who couldn't use his hands! He better pray they get to him before I do!! Bro is dead J, Ricky's f***king dead!!", Joey was hysterically crying on the phone. "Bro I warned yall, get out for them babies' sake. The streets don't love you, this is proof, please get out." We cried together on that phone for a long time. "When are you coming out here?" he asked. "Soon Bro, I have to see what I can pull together." I began to pray; I had spent every last dollar getting into my apartment and yet my pride kicked in again. I tried every resource I was given out in Texas, but I called no one back home to let them know with time that nothing had come through. "What time will you be getting here today?" Joey called to ask. "Bro I've tried everything, and nothing came through yet, I'm waiting for an answer from one more place and if they say no, I won't be able to make it." It crushed me to say those words. My brother cussed me out and rightfully so, I should've called and asked, now the tickets were too high and reality set in, I really was not going to make it to his funeral, this was crazy.

A LETTER TO MY BRO R.I.P

Bro I have barely gotten any sleep,

Since hearing of your departure to your spiritual retreat,

Now all I can do is reminisce on the memories of playing hide and seek,

Getting together for holidays and birthday parties,

Let's not forget that long trip in the mini-RV, down to Florida to visit Disney with Abuelo and Abuela.

You went from a young boy to a grown man,

Since birth God had written your plan,

We may not agree,

Especially when we see you in the struggle just trying to provide for your babies.

The departure of your flesh has left me in tears,

Tears of relief that you are no longer suffering in this emotional prison called the streets.

Your soul has been released by our higher being.

I love and miss you Bro!!

By: Janet M. Viera

JANET, JOEY AND RICKY IS WHAT I REMEMBER GROWING UP. WE DIDN'T GROW UP LIKE COUSINS, WE GREW UP LIKE BROTHERS AND SISTERS

CHAPTER: 11

"The truth is healing doesn't mean the damage never existed. It means the damage no longer controls your life."

Shakrukh Khan

Less than two years after losing Pops, I was back to square one with Ricky transitioning, going through all the stages of grief they taught you about in college. In My grief journey I added 2 stages to the five, that was anxiety and healing. My anxiety would come up when I was struggling with not reacting to the grief. I just wanted to cry, Repetitive, compacted unhealed grief was only bound to show up in other ways. I really didn't how much more I thought I could fit inside.

On the morning of Tatyana's birthday, I woke up in a rush. We had a field trip planned to the Dallas Zoo and she had been looking forward to it since she found out I was chaperoning, and it was on her birthday. That morning I was brushing my teeth and took notice that I couldn't hold the water in my mouth. I happened to look into the mirror and noticed my whole left side of the face was drooping. As a nurse your skills go straight signs of stroke, however I had no chest pains, my BP was normal, my O2 was normal, my pulse is a little elevated but that's to be expected considering I just scared the hell out of myself, lol. Ok everything is pretty much normal, if I go to the ER, they are going to send me home. I'll deal when we get home from the trip, it was her birthday and putting a smile on my kids faces meant more to me.

Attending the field trip prove to be a little more challenging than I expected. It was hot so I couldn't wear a hoodie to cover my crooked face. I had to bear the stares of like if I was playing the star role of Darkman. When we had a lunch break, two parents were brave enough to approach me, sit down and ask me was everything ok as opposed to staring. I explained to them what happened, I don't know, I mean I may know because I'm a nurse, but because I'm a nurse I can't self-diagnose. Yes, it's true I am one of the stubborn ones that waits until last minute, to realize her symptoms are more serious than she had ultimately assessed the situation or more, so she was ignoring them for not wanting to leave her babies until she has no other alternate options but to call 911. I was her; she was me.

Cracking jokes on myself, is what I learned when I was uncomfortable. Abuelo would say to us as kids, "Dile, ha, ha, ha, ha, ha," and he would let out one of those mariachis screams with each one. Then you would here Abuela, "Aye Viera callarte ese traqueteo!" as she made that crazy looking face towards us kids to get us laughing. That laughing at awkward moments got me in a load of trouble. Those memories are soul food to the body.

To get back on track, hey it happens, lol. I went to the doctors often, I took my meds like I was supposed, I had no other concerns except the pain in my heart that no one could fix but me. I had gained yet another guardian angel and didn't really talk about it much, once again. I felt the guilt of losing him to the streets and not making it to his service. I could feel little spits of hot water slowly boiling over in my pot, yet I ignored it. I would cry then snap out of it. I didn't allow myself those truly vulnerable moments as I know I should. Suck it up buttercup, you got this.

Pan African was introduced to us, and we began keeping ourselves entertained at various events they held. It was a dope vibe like I felt in Philly. So much wisdom and I was able to share this with my kids. Festivals galore, parades, pop up shops, 2014 was a pretty busy year attempting to keep the top tightly sealed on the boiling pot.

Losing weight at a rapid rate, pushing myself past my limits, insomnia, nightmares of him laying out there alone. Breathe Janet, you can do this. I was still attending church regularly, praying, reading my bible, talking to my Abuelos. I felt like I was deteriorating, he was too young.

His one-year anniversary came around the corner quick, I had just left there in early January. Being there was where I faced the reality that he was really gone. Not seeing his face, was heavy on my heart. My brother Joey really spent almost the whole time coming to see me while we were here. He was living in NY. We got to talking deep and I realized Bro really was trying to do better. Or he got better at hiding it.

Five days after I left, I received a phone call. that made the boiling pot explode and threw me off my rocker for a long time. Sitting at the Walmart on Forest Lane in Dallas, TX I received the news. My brother Joey was found unresponsive in a motel bathroom in Wildwood, NJ. "Janet, are you ok, please go home, are you ok?" my mom repeated. "Mom I'll be ok." I answered.

We just passed the one-year anniversary of Ricky's transition. We had just spoke now 4 days later you were gone?!?! I hung up the phone and then kept looking at it, ok mom calls me back tell me its another crazy joke Joey is playing. You know he was full of them. Ok Bro come on call me. Waiting for the phone to ring to tell me it was a joke, where was that phone call??? I became more anxious as minutes passed. I called around, "Put my brother on the phone! Tell him this shit isn't funny anymore!" "He's gone Cuz…." he responded. "Make sure Mommy is good." I hung up the phone and utterly lost it. I got back to my house, everything and anything that was glass was broken. I was screaming, crying, cussing God out, how could I trust him when he kept taking away everyone who was supposed to protect me. Leave me the hell alone, I'm done.

"He's not going to leave you alone, now open this door and let me in. Child what is going on? It sounded like you were fighting with someone over here, this was all you, baaaabbbbyyyy remind me not to piss you off." My neighbor said. She grabbed my broom and began sweeping up all the glass, it was getting close to the time to pick up the kids and I had to get it together. She told me go take a shower, get myself together and she would pick up the kids. She cooked dinner and stayed until the kids were in bed.

I was blessed with some great people in my life, all at the right time. I was able to get to NJ within no time and I will forever be grateful for every last one of you who were there. The ride home from the airport seemed to take forever and when we pulled in, I was hesitant to get out the car. Everyone began coming outside. I had no intentions on facing this funeral sober either. I ended up in NJ for 2 weeks due to the snow we had to postpone the services. It had been a little time, so I was back to being a lightweight, 2 shots easily covered up and I was nice. I stood at his casket with my legs feeling like rubber. Another box closed on another Viera face. How did my grandparents do this? Two sons and two grandsons.

I wanted to get back home so bad yet at the same time I didn't want to leave my family. I feared hugging one of them for the last time. When I got back to TX, I became a hermit. I spent almost a whole year in bed. I was depressed, could barely function. I would push myself to get up every morning to get my kids off to school. Would come back home and back to bed I would go until it was about time to pick them up, I would get myself together, put the mommy mask back on and play the role for a few hours. Homework, dinner, we would go to church on Sundays simply to check off a box and because my kids loved going. I felt distant. I would zone off.

A friend of mine kept coming out to invite us to her church. She reminded me of my Titi Titina, every week, come to church with me, I know you would love it. I didn't like mega churches, I felt lost in them. Did I mention she was smart as hell like Titi too? She comes in and asks, "Hey what are you doing Sunday evening around like 5p?" I'm thinking 5 pm all church services are done by then. "Nothing mama, church, park, dinner, just a regular ole Sunday." "Ok good we are all getting together and heading over to my church, we added a 5pm service now." She smiled. "You know what, I'll be there." I replied. I really did not want to go. Mega churches are mega headaches. But I told her I would so I'm going.

The parking lot was packed, it was a race to get the kids registered and get into the worship hall in time. After worship and introductions, the pastor comes on and begins his sermon. Dude looks young and he's dressed comfortably. Ok I see it's one of them churches, "Amen" I yelled, and I clapped my hands in praise. That Amen echoed through that huge quiet hall. OOOppppsss guess it's not one of them churches. I sat quietly and open the program, inside was everything I had been looking for, for years. My attention was interrupted when I heard the pastor say, "We all have things that we struggle with, I still struggle with passing by a billboard and not staring at the woman half naked on there. I still struggle with watching porn." What the F**K, I covered my mouth, oohhhh God I apologize, that slipped but did this man just say that or was I hearing things? He repeated it and I looked stunned. Never in my entire life had I ever heard a pastor say they struggled with porn. I didn't know how to feel. The energy in that place was amazing, you felt it when you walked in however a pastor struggling with porn, that was different, and I had to ease into that.

The very next morning I walked into the grief ministry. I knew I was ready to unpack this pain. I made a commitment to make a change within myself. I returned that Tuesday evening being that they offered childcare at that time, and I found out they had grief classes for kids, I signed them up and we all took grief classes.

The following week I showed up on a Monday, they had women's groups, where we got together and worked through our various struggles. I walked into that worship hall, and I was early. I cried from the time I walked in there, until the time I walked out. It was such a peaceful feeling walking in there and tears were of gratitude. This is all I ever wanted, a safe environment to be vulnerable and not be judged on what I said, instead be directed.

God knew what he was doing when he kept sending my friend relentlessly. God knew why he was trying for months to get me out my bed and in that building. God knew exactly what he was doing all along.

It was not the end of my grief journey, this was the beginning of the most revealing yet rewarding years of my life, up until 2020. It would've been nice to know earlier, that the key to freedom was vulnerability. Speaking your story with confidence is key, it may unlock the prison in someone else's mind.

MISC # THANK YOU POEM

IVE FINALLY SORTED THIS CONFUSION OUT SO I CAN TELL MY STORY

MY STORY OF HOW MY HEART WAS FILLED WITH FURY

FURY THAT TURNED INTO SADNESS

SADNESS THAT TURNED INTO HURT

HURT THAT TURNED INTO TEARS

AS I FREED MYSELF ONE BY ONE OF ALL THE BAGGAGE IVE COLLECTED OVER THE YEARS

VANISHING MY FEARS

STEP BY STEP WITH EACH TEAR

SHEDDING MY SKIN

GROWING A NEW ONE

NO ONE SAID LIVING LIFE WAS GOING TO BE ALL FUN

BUT MAN, ALL THESE BAGS WERE BLOCKING THE SUN

BEING A REAL WOMAN

REALIZING MY WORTH

LEARNING HOW TO NOT SETTLE FOR LESS

FINALLY PUTTING THESE RULES INTO PRACTICE IS WHAT HAS LED ME TO MY PERSONAL HAPPINESS AND SUCCESS.

IVE REALIZED THAT EVERYTHING IVE DONE IN MY LIFE HAS BEEN BY CHOICE AND NOT BECAUSE MY MIND HAS BEEN CARESSED

THANK YOU TO ALL THOSE WHO BROUGHT A TEAR TO MY EYE

THANK YOU TO ALL THOSE WHO HAVE PLACED A HURT IN MY HEART

THANK YOU TO ALL THOSE WHO TRIED TO TEAR ME APART AND ATTEMPT TO MAKE ME FEEL LIKE I WAS A DISGRACE

AND A SPECIAL THANK YOU TO THOSE WHO WERE THERE AND PUT A SMILE ON MY FACE

AND FOR ALL THOSE WHO TURNED THEIR BACKS, WHEN TIMES GOT TOUGH YOU JUST DISAPPEARED LIKE THAT,

YOU HAVE TO FACE THE COLD HARD FACTS THAT YOU ARE NO LONGER PRIVILEGED WITH BEING A PRESENCE IN MY LIFE

AND I'VE FORGIVEN YOU

KNOWLEDGE IS POWER.... BUT COMMUNICATION IS KEY

WITHOUT ALL THE LESSONS IVE LEARNED I WOULDN'T TO BE ABLE TO BE FREE TO BE ME.

I HAVE PICKED THE LOCKS.... I HAVE BROKE THE CHAINS

I HAVE FREED MYSELF FROM THE TEARS AND THE PAIN

I HAVE STOPPED THE RAIN AND UNBLOCKED THE SUN

I REMOVED THE BAGS ON MY BACK THEY FELT LIKE A TON

I FEEL LIKE IM FREE.... I FEEL LIKE IVE FINALLY WON

IN THE END LIFE IS NOTHING MORE THAN A NEVER-ENDING LESSON

THAT IS TAUGHT BY THE MAN IN THE HEAVENS ABOVE

WHO HAS BLESSED ME WITH A HEART FILLED WITH LOVE AND I CAN SAY NOTHING MORE THAN THANK YOU.

BY: Janet M. VIERA

PS from Janet:

This story doesn't end here, the best is yet to come Follow us at

Instagram: @poetrybehindprisonbars

Facebook: @poetrybehindprisonbars

To get updates on my next book being released titled #VieraStrong – Free At Last

Excerpt from upcoming book: #VieraStrong — Free At Last

"Lo hiciste. Él lo dijo y tú lo hiciste." Abuelo said. I looked at him a bit confused, however I quickly shrugged it off to his cancer and chemo. The excitement of getting my book cover done and being able to show my Abuelo and Abuela before they left this earth was an awesome feeling. I looked at him and seen, he was still staring at my phone and had the biggest smile on his face. "Estoy muy orgulloso de ustedes," he said. I was glowing and feeling like his little girl all over again.

It wasn't until after he transitioned that I found out what he meant by that beginning statement. My mind was blown, and tears of gratitude just flowed from my eyes………

It's not where I am, its where my thoughts ....Take US!

JOEY 92

Mom & Dad

Algun dia sere famoso, pues aguanta este "POSTER" 😊, que ussteds lo veran. "Your Son" JOEY 92

ABOUT THE AUTHOR

Janet is an optimistic poet, and author of this amazing book, Poetry Behind Prison Bars. The book embraces revitalizing poems by Janet's father who wrote some heart-warming and encouraging verses that stir the soul and bring in gratitude and positivity. Inspired by the wisdom and blessed with the writing gift, Janet continued the legacy of her father and her Abuela. She came into the world of writing and poetry which is also showcased in her book. Another great inspiration behind Janet's writing are historic poets such as Sonia Sanchez, Miguel Piñero, and Maya Angelou just to name a few.

Her father's period in jail and then the loss of her father while in jail, worked as a turning point in Janet's life. She experienced grief, depression, anxiety, and being a child who was never shown how to cope with her closest person's death. She utilized poetry to manage her emotions, and to heal herself after the loss of her dad, first to jail then to cancer. Although he never seen another free day while on earth, he always repeated the words to her, "It's not where I am, it's where my thoughts take us." Janet kept those words close to heart and decided she wants to use all of their poetry as a source of bringing peace, love, prayers and healing to the everyday life of people, as well as continuous healing to herself. With time, she spread her wings and started embracing life with gratitude, positivity, prayers, and meditation. Her expression of emotions and way of perceiving life may be life-saving for many people. Never held back, she continued spreading the word of auspiciousness and love through a Facebook page where people can connect, relate, share their experiences, and learn.

Her work is accredited by over 20+ years of healthcare experience caring for individuals ranging from children, to the disabled, to the beautiful old souls further proving that healing and bringing light to others has always been her purpose.

In addition to being the source of her creativity, her love of nature, meditation, praying, practicing gratitude are her strengths and resiliency is her super power. Her deepest thoughts come while sitting on her grandparents porch swing, inspired by the memories in the house she grew up in, she brings heart-touching pieces of poetry and short stories to paper.

To know more about Janet, the book, and her work, please visit:

Blog: www.poetrybehindprisonbars.com

Facebook Page: @PoetryBehindPrisonBars

Instagram: @PoetryBehindPrisonBars

Made in the USA
Middletown, DE
04 November 2021